Material Assumptions:
PAPER
AS DIALOGUE
June 15 – August 11, 2012

Curated by Jessica Cochran with Elizabeth Isakson-Dado, Hannah King and C.J. Mace*

WORKS FROM DIEU DONNÉ BY

Folly Apfelbaum
Sonya Blesofsky
Mel Bochner
Nina Bovasso
Beth Campbell
Chuck Close
Ian Cooper
Matt Keegan
William Kentridge
Glenn Ligon
Jessica Stockholder
Richard Tuttle

NEWLY COMMISSIONED WORKS BY

Deborah Boardman
Annica Cuppetelli & Cristobal Mendoza
Dan Devening
Susan Goethel Campbell
Daniel Luedtke
Niall McClelland
Kate McQuillen
Zoe Nelson
Julie Schenkelberg
Ian Schneller
Matthew Shlian
Anna Tsantir

Center for Book & Paper Arts Staff

Steve Woodall, Director
Gina Ordaz, Assistant to the Director
Jessica Cochran, Curator of Exhibitions & Programs
April Sheridan, Studio Technician & Special Events Coordinator
Brad Freeman, Studio Coordinator & Editor, Journal of Artists' Books
Tracey Drobot, Administrative Assistant
Jeremy Jennings, Gallery Assistant
Caitlin O'Meara, Gallery Assistant

EXHIBITION SUPPORT
Susan Green, Copy Editor
John Boehm, Photographer

Special thanks to Lauren Shaw, Dieu Donné for curatorial support, and Trisha Martin and Boo Gilder for paper production assistance.

* The exhibition was organized as part of a curatorial studies independent study in the Interdisciplinary Arts Department, led by Melissa Potter, Acting Director, Book & Paper Program and Jessica Cochran, Curator of Exhibitions.

0-929911-44-X

Published in 2012. First edition.

The Center for Book and Paper Arts at Columbia College Chicago
1104 South Wabash Avenue
Chicago, Illinois 60605-1996, U.S.A.

www.colum.edu/bookandpaper

BOOK
AND PAPER
CENTER FOR BOOK AND PAPER ARTS
at Columbia College Chicago

DIEU /
DONNÉ
/

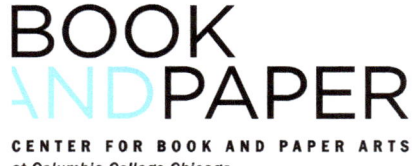

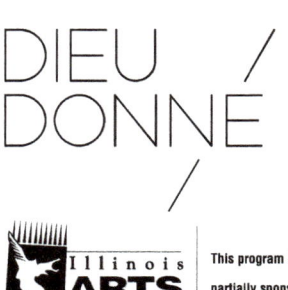

This program is partially sponsored by a grant from the Illinois Arts Council

Material Assumptions:
PAPER
AS DIALOGUE

CONTENTS

CURATING AS PEDAGOGY, PAPER AS DIALOGUE

Jessica Cochran

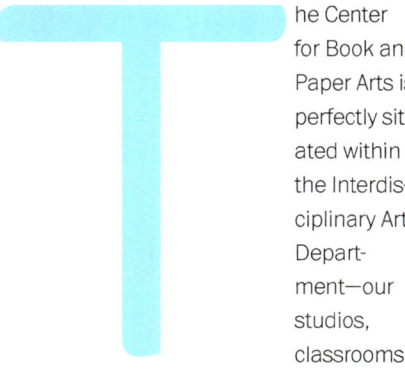

The Center for Book and Paper Arts is perfectly situated within the Interdisciplinary Arts Department—our studios, classrooms, gallery, and offices steadily hum with graduate student and faculty activity; it is an energizing atmosphere, and we are happy to harness not only the students' enthusiasm, but also their ideas and growing expertise. In January 2012, Assistant Professor Melissa Potter and I initiated an independent study opportunity, for which graduate students could receive three credits for assisting me in the organization of our summer exhibition. From curatorial concept to marketing and installation, each student was granted creative agency in every stage of the process.

I curated *Material Assumptions: Paper as Dialogue* with assistance from Elizabeth Isakson-Dado (MFA '13), C. J. Mace (MFA '12), and Hannah King (MFA '13). Split into two sections, *Material Assumptions* features works in handmade paper by prominent artists made while in residence at Dieu Donné. For the second section, we commissioned thirteen interdisciplinary artists to create new works out of paper hand made in our studios. Because we have placed hand-made paper into the hands of visual artists for whom paper (much less handmade paper) may not be a primary medium, the exhibition asks us to consider that "handmadeness points not to a certain visual or aesthetic trope, but to realms of possibility."

Consulting with each artist, the curatorial assistants not only produced the paper, but also worked one-on-one with artists to determine the types, sizes, and fibers best suited to each project. In this model, knowledge flows both ways: our students are uniquely poised to share their sophisticated understanding of paper with contemporary artists; in turn they glean from each artist yet a new way the practice of hand papermaking can translate provocatively and meaningfully into ever-wider realms of art production and discourse.

Artists have long immersed themselves in the practice of exhibition making through the creation of artist-run spaces. Increasingly, however, artists are feeling comfortable adapting more explicitly curatorial roles, within both an aesthetic and a professional dimension, hence the ubiquity of the term, "artist as curator."

To that end, the impetus for adding a pedagogical layer to our exhibitions at the Center for Book and Paper Arts is as much about professional development for our graduate students as it is about artistic growth: professionally, exhibitions are an important public vehicle for display, communication, and education, as we work to "center" hand papermaking within the field of interdisciplinary arts discourse. But for an artist working today, how can the collaborative act of curating someone else's project translate into a more nuanced consideration of the way one's own work exists in the white cube—and then in the world beyond it?

In a 2011 lecture called "On Curatorial Intelligence", curator Kitty Scott identified what she considers ten best practices for working curators. Situated among suggestions about collection building and international research, there were several points that resonated strongly in relation to this project:

> Work closely with the artist and provide them with the best conditions possible for their work; listen to them and protect their vision.
>
> Remain open and curious, but at the same time, maintain a critical attitude.
>
> Follow intuition; take risks. Support new work by emerging artists.
>
> Be transparent when teaching others about curating; be prepared to reveal feelings of doubt and complexity.

Generative exhibitions like this one, those that result in the production of new works, are essentially rooted in an "open and curious" approach meant to provide artists

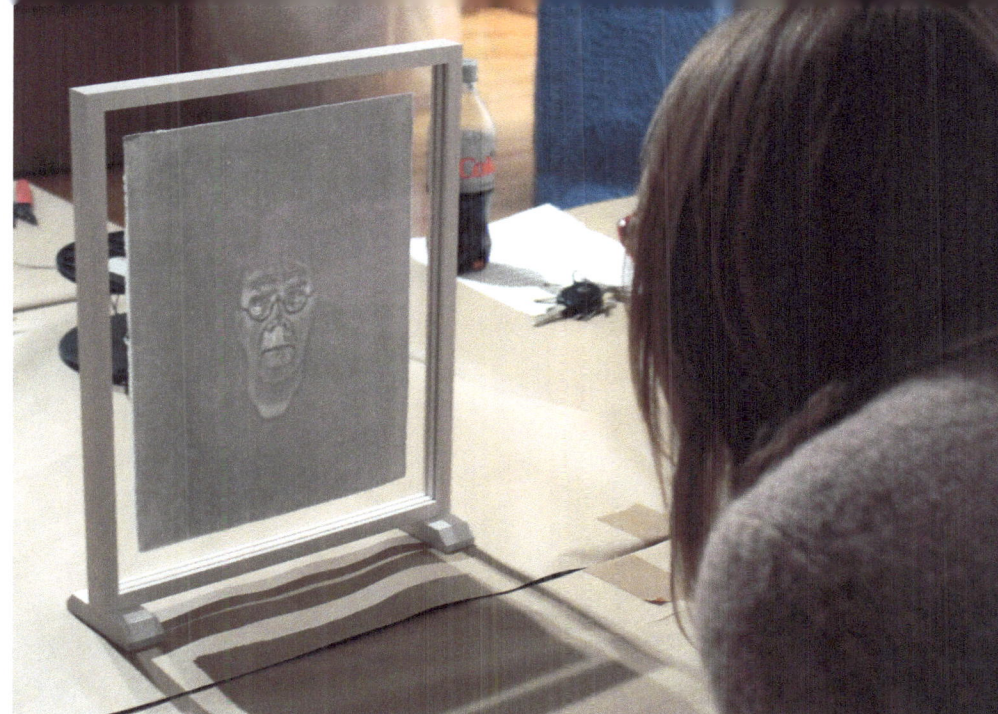

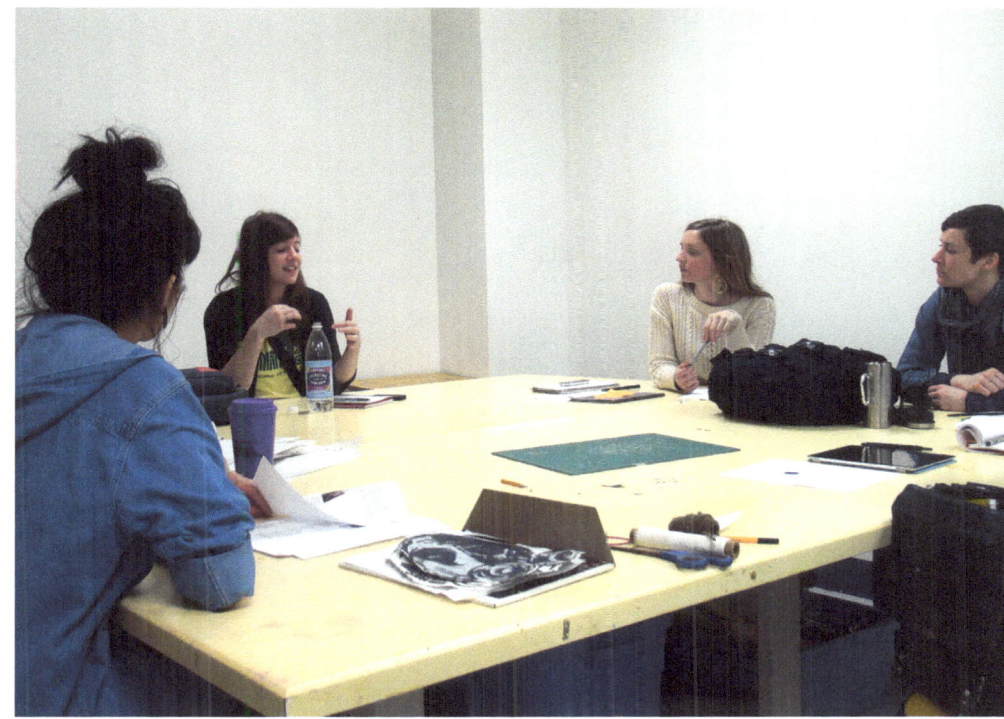

with the "best possible conditions" for their vision. At the same time, they leave ample room for chance, and in the process they complicate the role of the curators. Ranging from the most practical of potential issues to the more philosophical ones, we inevitably find ourselves asking—in what Scott identifies as moments of "doubt and complexity"—Will each artist feel satisfied with her contribution? Will the resulting projects work cohesively within the space? What if the finished works feel unresolved, or unfinished?

The same space, however, that allows for small failures and insecurity on the side of both curator and artist, also provides room for the extraordinary. As I write this, the works have not yet been finished, and they will not arrive to the gallery for weeks. Artists' reports from the studios however, reveal works in progress that are fascinating and relevant. At present, Kate McQuillen is creating haunting, yet ineffable print transfers of fake weapons sewn into her clothes, in order to express what she considers her "absurd" fears of being suspected a terrorist. Here the handmade paper serves as an experimental printing surface for the artist as she reaches for unexpected aesthetic effects. In her project *Other Cities*, Susan Goethel Campbell, is currently generating black-and-white relief prints based on aerial views of cities at night and patterns of urbanization. According to the artist, the handmade paper plays an "important role" as the "object and carrier of the illusion of

space," as "subtle gray values draw from atmospheric phenomena and make use of unique grain patterns found in the woodblock from which the pieces were printed."

The Center for Book and Paper Arts, like countless small alternative spaces, community arts centers, and research-driven academic galleries, is a center that exists at a margin. We promote and teach complex practices that are often difficult to classify,

and are non market-driven and under-recognized by the art world. As such, it is our responsibility to create and offer models for exhibitions that foster experimental and horizontal flows of knowledge. In this case, from curator to student, student to artist, and artist back to student, we have realized a productive dynamic in which, no matter how successful the final exhibition, the process is the outcome.

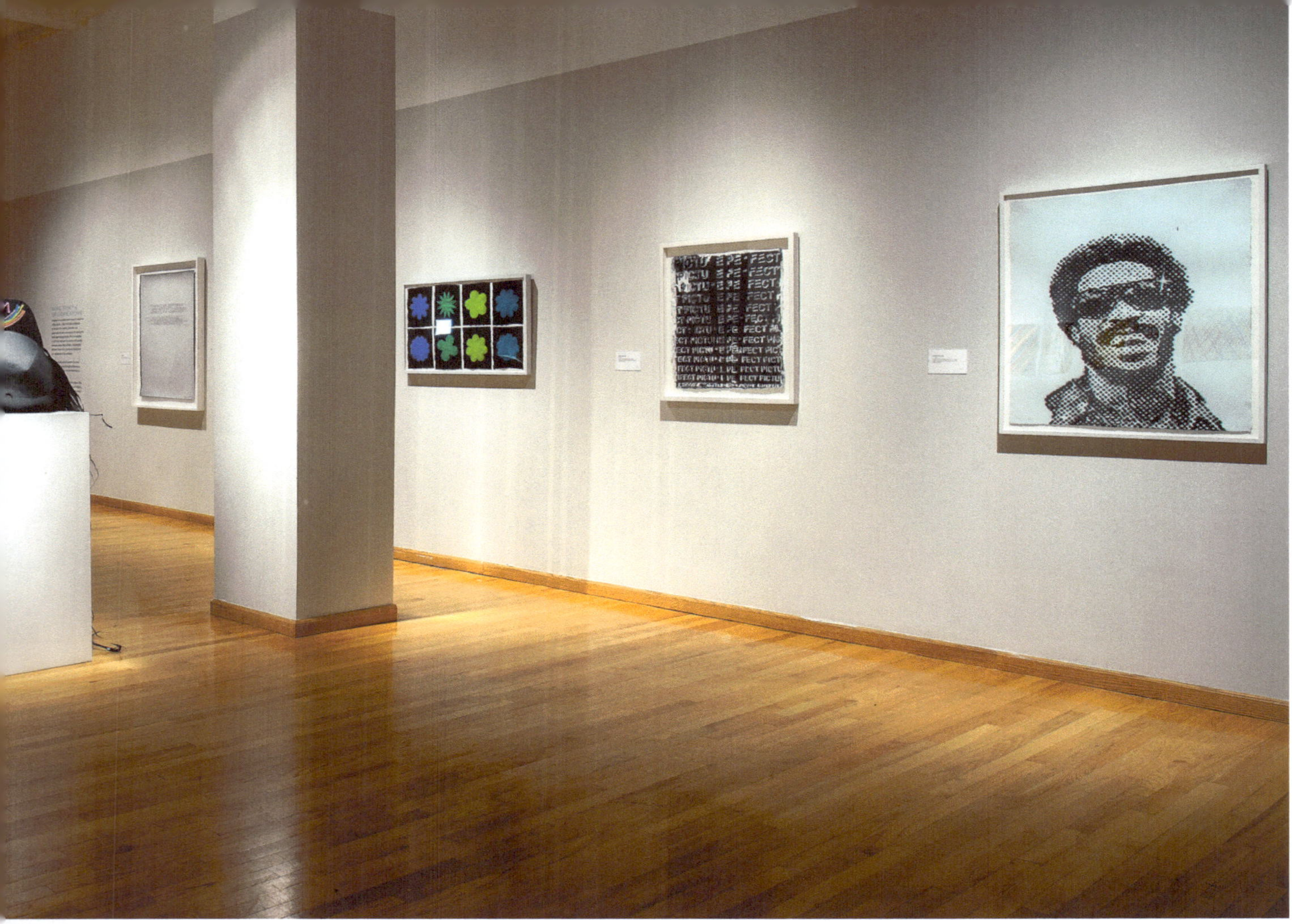

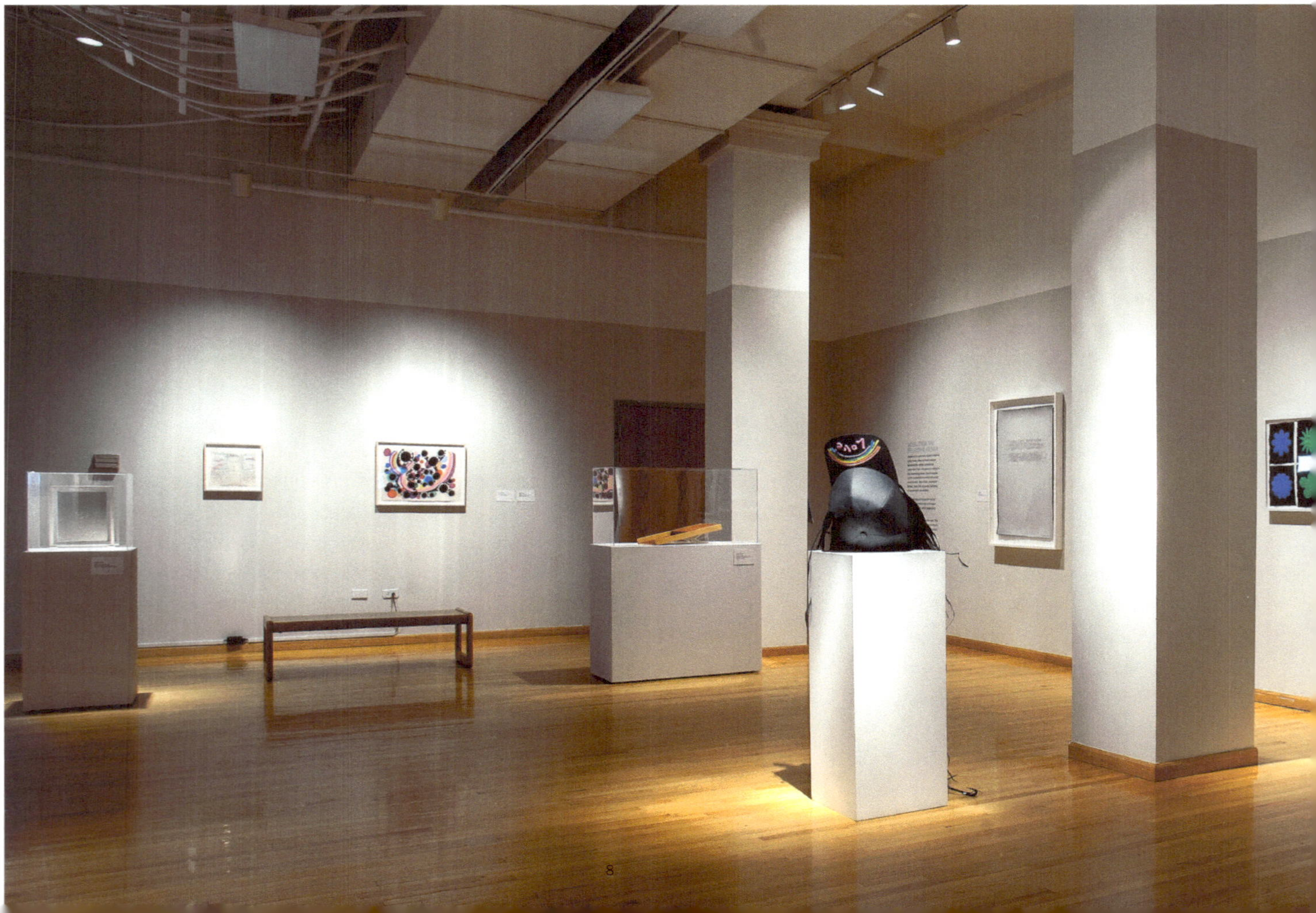

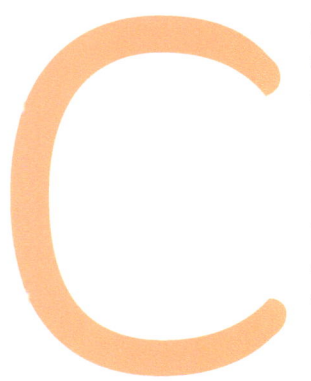 olumbia College Chicago's Interdisciplinary Arts Department is thrilled to collaborate with Dieu Donné Papermill on our summer 2012 exhibition, *Material Assumptions: Paper as Dialogue*. To create an interdisciplinary learning opportunity, curator of exhibitions and programs for the Columbia College Chicago Center for Book and Paper Arts, Jessica Cochran, and I created a credit-bearing course for three current Book and Paper MFA candidates: Hannah King, Elizabeth Isakson-Dado, and C. J. Mace. They participated in all aspects of the exhibition including curation, direction, and hand papermaking production for exhibiting artists. Book and Paper program MFA thesis candidate, Trisha Martin, generously donated her time and outstanding papermaking skills to the project as well.

The project engages the mission of the Interdisciplinary Arts Department, which encourages students to consider art in its relationship to practices including collaboration, discourse building, and education.

In the evolving contemporary art landscape, this approach offers new ways to shape and define the book and paper arts, and to consider their importance not only in cultural production, but also in historical and social contexts.

Interdisciplinary Arts students produced handmade paper reflecting the aesthetic and conceptual concerns of thirteen individual artists featured in the exhibition. The projects range from large-scale translucent papers made from specialized fibers like abaca (a member of the banana plant family), to laminated cotton sheets with the thickness of chipboard. The work presents hand papermaking collaboration as an artistic exercise in and of itself, one in which the collaborator challenges us to consider where, how, and at what moment art is made through her ability to conceptualize and interpret in this medium. This paper production also highlights the possibilities of the Center's beautiful and well-equipped papermaking studio, one of just a few of its kind in the world.

As part of student participation in the curatorial and organizational aspects of the exhibition, students created a blog and wrote curatorial essays featuring their experiences with the process, as well as theoretical and philosophical aspects

related to the exhibition and their own work in the medium. Their work deepens the discourse in the field at large at a historical moment in which the relevance of analog artistic practice is considered in relation to digital media.

It has been remarkable to watch students explore paper production, curation, and exhibition planning as extensions of their interdisciplinary art practice. A number of years before her untimely passing, Center for Book and Paper Arts founder, Marilyn Sward, worked with Dieu Donné founder, Sue Gosin, and me on a program called the Master Papermaking Fellowship. It was a program intended to preserve and promote the hand papermaking medium as an art form through master and apprentice relationships at flagship studios throughout the country including both Dieu Donné and Columbia College Chicago. This project extends Marilyn's dream for the Center and the field at large, and we are all tremendously proud to carry on that legacy with this remarkable exhibition opportunity.

Melissa Potter
Acting Director and Assistant Professor,
Book & Paper Program,
Columbia College Chicago
April 2012

CRAFTING ENCOUNTERS: PAPERMAKING AND MAKER CULTURE IN CONTEMPORARY MEDIA

C.J. Mace

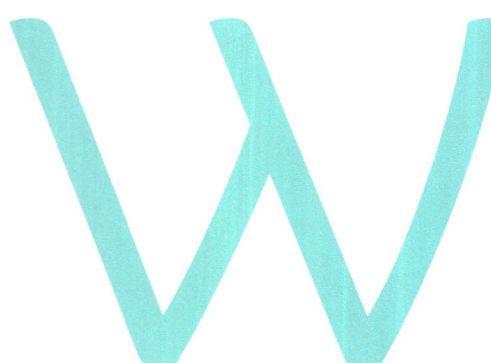

hen critics and theorists attempt to define craft, *refinement* or *skill* is often a part of the definition, as well as a focus on the resulting object. The thought is that we read the handiwork and see time and mastery. The object supposedly points to its maker in this way. Yet any refinement requires practice and prototype, apprenticeship and exchange, experiment and failure, and, increasingly, collective processes or collaborative fabrication. The object has little or no meaning as an end in itself, and the line between industrial and handmade is blurry at best. This makes it nearly impossible to use handiwork as a defining characteristic of craft.

Material Assumptions explores the way this focus challenges how we delineate community, assign value, and see accomplishment and failure in larger culture. Artists drive the process of making but often have not had the resources or power to frame the "final" work; in response, many have adopted prototypes and participatory making as their focus instead of seeing them as by-products. Objects are made in constant processes of activation, recreation, and reiteration, both in the process that got the object there and in the continued enactment of, reception of, and performance with/of/around the object. They are a way to open a space for thinking, contact, and acting. Informed by new media theory, this show positions craft as an orientation to making and enacting within contemporary art instead of an origination; as a media technology, what paper "means" fluxes, co-exists, rises, falls, and re-emerges in cultural history.

While remaining very clear about my role as curator and not artist in this instance, I see this curatorial project as an extension of my personal practice. Handmade paper is a particularly expressive and challenging method of communication and dissemination. We curators are playing a unique role in that we are also making the paper for the artists: we can make it to specifications for them, it is easily sent and transported, and it suits a variety of approaches and practices. Most importantly, the project provokes all of us to talk about why and how we are using it. Part of the endeavor is the translation between technical language and creative vision. The goal of this project is not to find what is unique to works with paper but use it as a productive restriction and a point of contact with the artists we have commissioned.

REUSE / REMAKE / RESEND

Material Assumptions roots papermaking firmly in broader "maker culture," embracing mediums not commonly thought of as traditional craft mediums. As the artists that intrigue me personally span across various media and fields, one way I think of paper is as a component technology that gets shared. Ian Cooper, in his statement about the pieces he created for the Dieu Donné Workspace Program, writes that the source materials feeding his practice include "poor quality paparazzi photograph[s]," "coming of age films and television programs," and other pop culture forms that thrive on endless loops of rumor and self-reference. By describing his process of making as "reconfiguring"

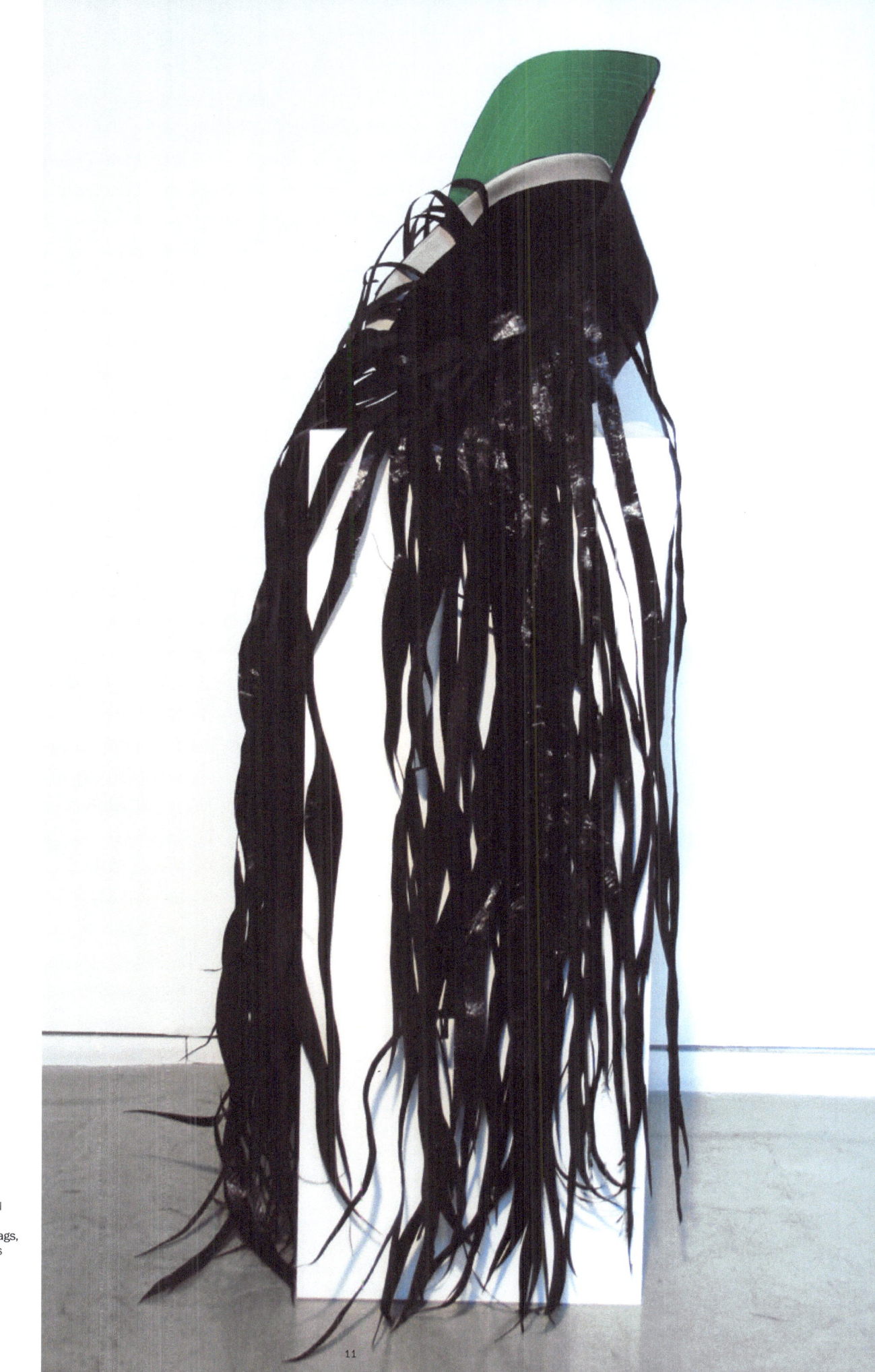

IAN COOPER *Chalice*,
2010. Handmade
denim and cotton
papers, commercial
papers, fabric, cast
paper pulp, trash bags,
brush bristles, gloss
medium, and Jade
adhesive. Courtesy
Dieu Donné.

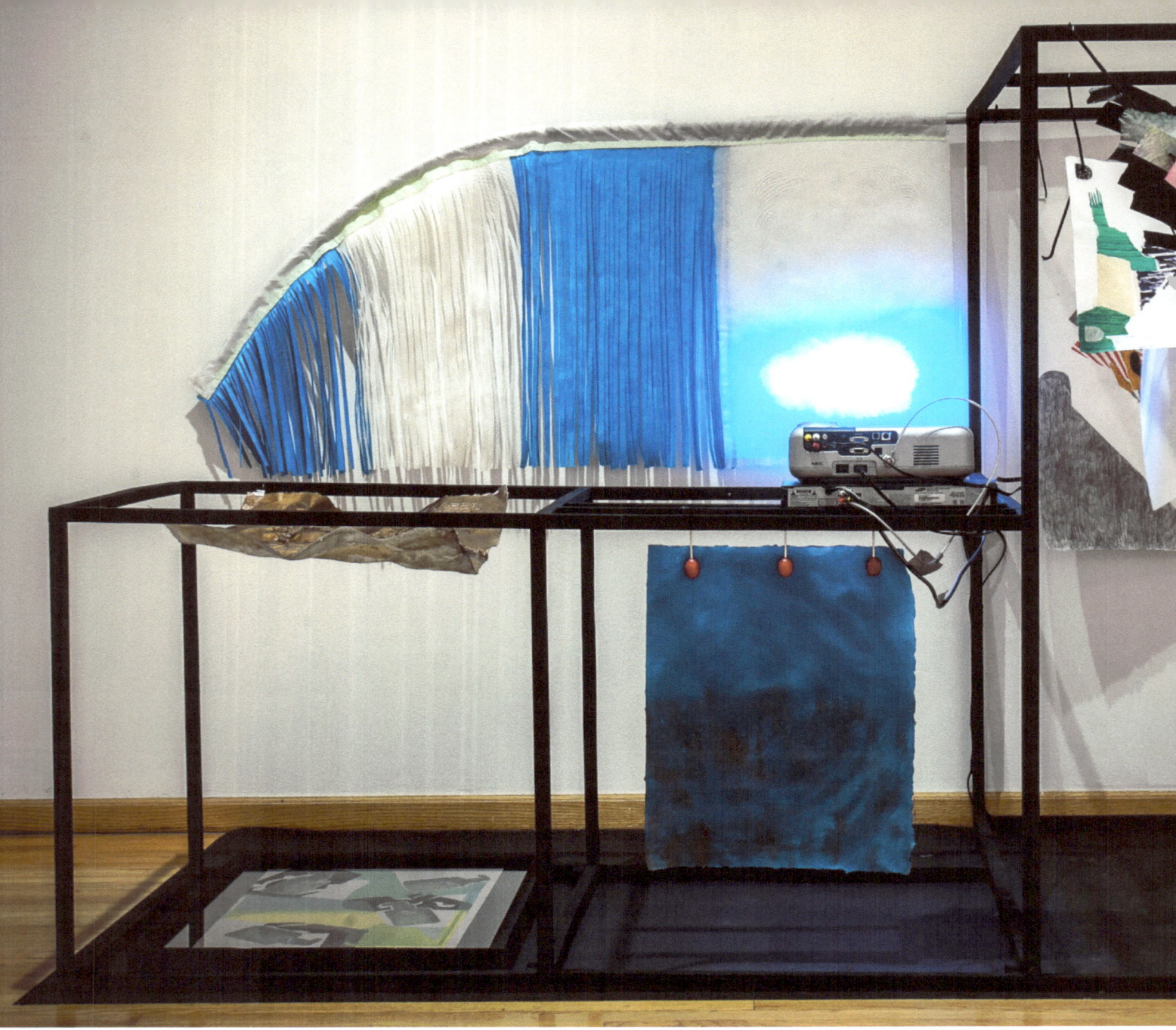

and "extracting," he acknowledges this referential bricolage—the lineage of pop culture associations that feed his work. Defined by cascading streams of allusion, *craft* becomes focused on dissemination and flexibility instead of exactness or authenticity. His 2010 sculpture, *Chalice*, for example, combines handmade papers with such materials as trash bags, fabric, and commercial paper. His residence in the Dieu Donné Workspace Program demonstrates how makers build creative community, not around materials or processes, but around modes of inquiry and approaches to experimental producing which may or may not be completely "handmade."

COMPONENT DESIRES

The laborious processes that often characterize and help define craft are really encounters, acts that make desires manifest in some concrete way as catalysts for the dialogue between us. "Handmade" is just one way to symbolize not so much the labor of the handiwork but a labor to connect made physical. These objects are a social interface; their design, the materials used, the way they are presented matter, but these qualities matter because they shape how we communicate, connect, and access meaning. Paper is a modular, malleable substance that has limitations and conventions of use. These conventions are pushed, stretched, and utterly broken by the artists, who may have no investment in the fact that it is handmade.

In activating the assumption that objects imply makers, many makers are often crafting an image or persona via their work, making a performance out of that work. This image may not be polished; it may be purposefully de-skilled, awkward, ugly, weird, uncomfortable, repulsive,

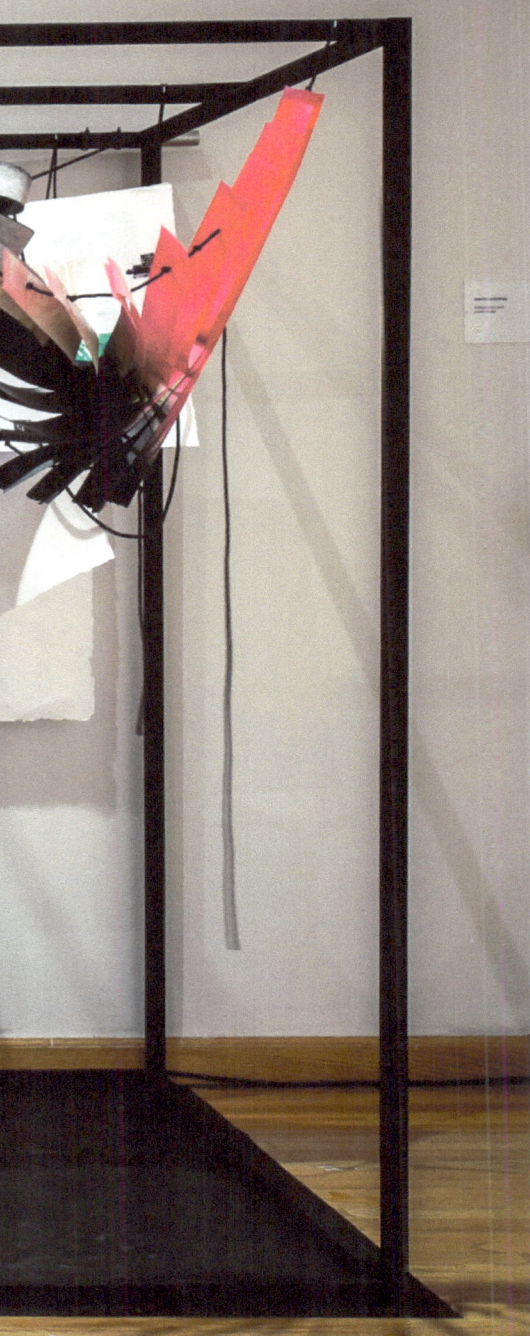

DANIEL LUEDTKE *Birthday Girl*, 2012. Mixed media installation. Dimensions variable.

of his ability. These instructions could be nonsensical, impractical, conceptual, poetic, or completely deadpan. His chosen responsibility was to fulfill our desires through the object he produced in response to those instructions, subverting a hierarchy of producer and receiver. He looks at craft in terms of desire, trust, fulfillment, and utopian yearnings enacted into the world via both the object and the ritual making of the object.

Larger remix culture has relevance within papermaking, infusing it with a sense of "impreciousness" and expandable expendability. This sense can butt heads with the laboriousness of production and the need for physical space and resources that often accompanies making. It also contradicts efforts to find authenticity or read the object as a manifestation of the identity of the maker. In this line of thinking, the object becomes a cipher instead of a glyph, with shifting significances and relevancies. The goal is not to devalue the labor of making but to emphasize its value within a larger system of making meaning.

In my own work, I approach the objects I make as just the first point of contact, the "hook" that draws participants in. I work extensively in prototypes, assuming that the artwork only exists as others use and test it, feeding its lifespan with videos, pictures, and accounts of how it was used. Awkwardness can serve a purpose, as can ugliness and wear. *Refinement*, in my practice, does not mean *finish*; it means thinking extensively how participants will read and use what I make. It means seeing the gallery as a test space where participants activate the artwork. It means a series of projects in conversation. Studio and gallery often cease to be separate spaces.

"Studio" has become a dispersed and mobile idea, even when the particular processes one utilizes may require

significant space and equipment, as does papermaking. Like the open source movement in software, many makers now participate in dispersed, collaborative communities, where part of the craft is organizing situational creativity. They may use the object merely as a locus of participation or as the artifact of a performance; they may source some of the hand work elsewhere; they may use materials previously thought of as industrial or they may focus on the intense, repetitive labor of their process, the system they create each time they make, over the quality of the actual materials used.

CONCLUSION

The papermaking studio is a key nodal site in a series of exchanges that may or may not become an artwork; it is also a testing ground and research site. This is abundantly evident from the cross-section of artists who have chosen to participate in this project: printmakers, installation artists, hybrid media artists, a paper engineer, and an instrument maker are just part of the list. Vibrant communities are built around a variety of levels of investment because that investment shapes the networks that get built.

Papermaking is important precisely because it is not precious; that is, its value comes from knowledge and skill sharing not reserving or preserving. It, as a material, should be treated carelessly in order to learn the most about its potential as a medium. Studio practice must adapt to this reality. Instead of re-enforcing dichotomies between industrial and handmade, analog and digital, or made and produced, papermaking as remix refocuses the conversation, positing making as a participatory and communicative action that has the concrete side effect of marshaling resources and carving out necessary spaces for exchange. At stake is our worldviews, how we make and define ourselves through these exchanges.

or lo-fi. It also contradicts objects as a boundary policing "source" of identity while acknowledging we craft identity in an ongoing process partly through the objects and artifacts we make.

Daniel Luedtke, one of the artists commissioned to produce new work, makes fluidity and communicative potential the focus of his work. He proposed that we make both the paper and the instructions for its use, even drawing or writing instructions on or inside the paper. His job, then, was to produce pieces that completed those instructions to the best

SUSAN GOETHEL CAMPBELL

My installation, *Other Cities*, is a series of black-and-white relief prints based on aerial views of cities at night and patterns of urbanization. The work stems from my interest in atmospheric phenomena, the experience of flying and the geometry of cities at night as seen from above. Several images for the installation draw from video stills I shot from airplanes. I have arranged the prints in clusters, reflecting how low cloud ceilings reveal and conceal the ground plane below.

Some groups of very dark prints in the installation contain linear elements comprised of hundreds of tiny hand-punched holes. The holes read as patterns of light and reflect how networks of roads and the geometry of dense urban centers glow at night when seen from above. The prints are scattered across the wall at different heights. Many works form contiguous relationships by linking lines, points, and angles to create an overall impression of a sprawling metropolis.

The handmade paper plays an important role in the installation of prints. It is both object and carrier of the illusion of space. Several sheets contain printed gradations of tonal fields and nothing else. These subtle gray values draw from atmospheric phenomena and make use of unique grain patterns found in the woodblock from which the pieces were printed. When interspersed with the perforated prints, the continuous tonal fields provide a strong contrast from the hard geometry of the perforated pieces. When moving through the print installation, these minimal works act like a low cloud ceiling by concealing information. The paper becomes objectified, emphasizing the organic geometry and irregularity of the hand-made paper.

Overall, *Other Cities* plays with the relationship between the natural and the artificial. The handmade paper as a support contributes to this idea. Imperfections in the paper bring a humanistic element to the macroscopic views of the engineered environment. The organic rectangle of the sheet of paper made from natural fibers underscores, for me, the role the hand can play in shaping one's environment.

Susan Goethel Campbell has exhibited in solo and group exhibitions nationally and internationally, including The Drawing Center and the International Print Center in New York. Solo exhibitions include the Academy of Merksem, Antwerp, Belgium; Kathryn Markel, New York; and Lemberg Gallery, Ferndale, Michigan. Susan is the recipient of a 2009 Kresge Artist Fellowship; a 2008 printmaking residency at the Flemish Center for Graphic Arts in Kasterlee, Belgium; and the Beisinghoff Printmaking Residency in Diemelstadt-Rhoden, Germany, in 2012. Her work is in private and public collections including the National Museum of Women in the Arts, New York Public Library, Detroit Institute of Arts, Toledo Museum of Art, and the University of Michigan Special Collections Library. Susan earned a MFA in printmaking from Cranbrook Academy of Art.

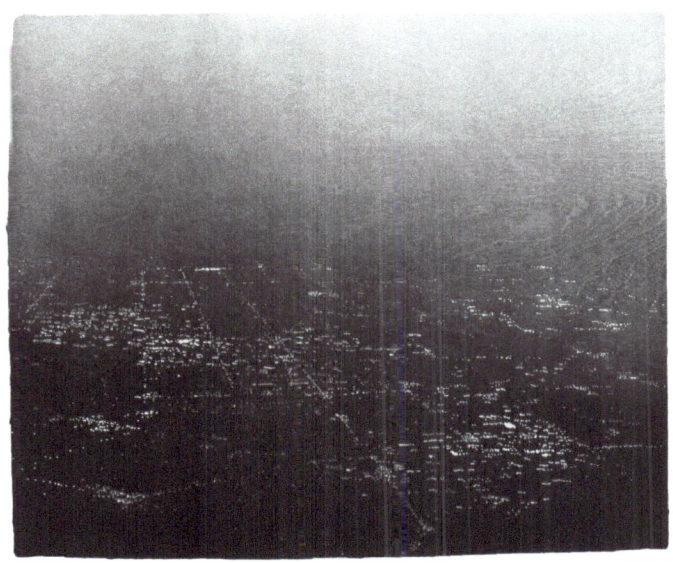 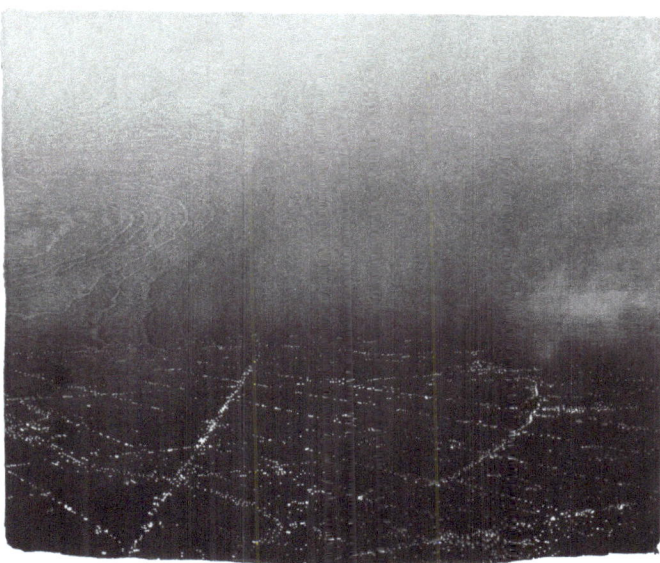

SUSAN GOETHEL CAMPBELL *Other Cities 1 & 2,* 2012. Relief print with perforations on handmade cotton paper. 20 x 24 inches each. Unique.

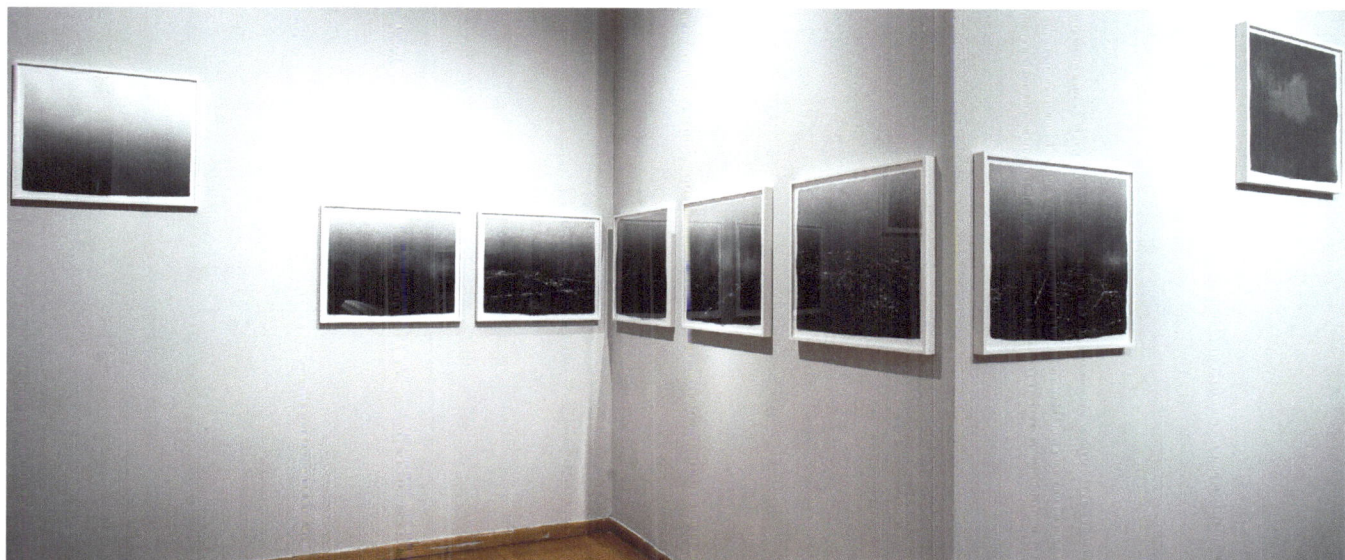

SUSAN GOETHEL CAMPBELL *Other Cities 1–10,* (installation view) 2012. Relief print with perforations on handmade cotton paper. 20 x 24 inches each. Unique.

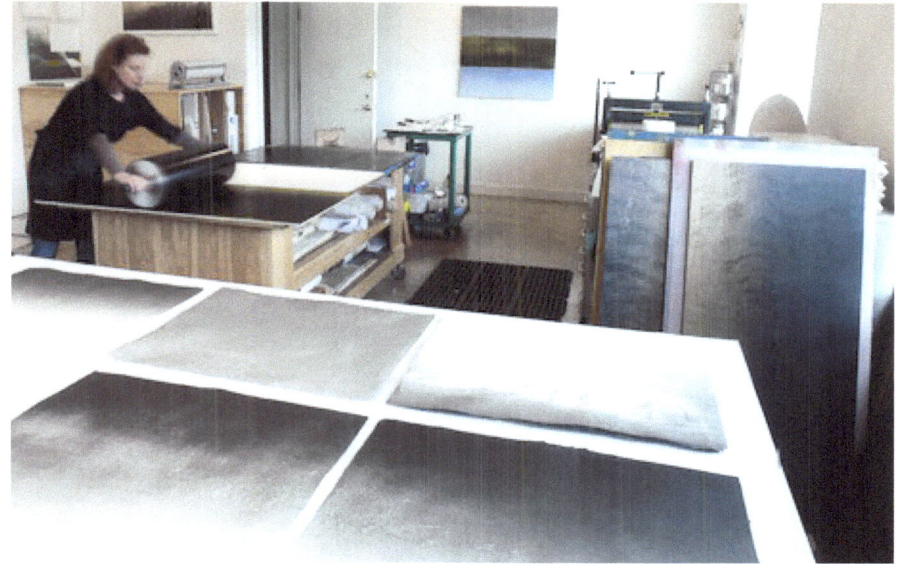

SUSAN GOETHEL CAMPBELL in her studio, Detroit. Photo by Tim Thayer.

ZOE NELSON

I'm interested in subverting the historical function of paper as a surface for the word by acknowledging the process of making handmade paper, playing with the medium's tactility, and turning it into a sculptural object. Historically, paper has been used to organize language and thoughts, sacrificing its own tactile "paper-ness" for the sake of the word. I am interested in the possibility of paper as negative space, as the area in between language, as opposed to that which makes language legible and coherent. For this reason, my project attempts to resurrect the paper-ness of paper by turning it into a three-dimensional object removed from its linguistic utility. What is interesting is that in our age of technology, paper has arguably become even less functional as the printed word is dying. I find the paper object to be particularly awkward and funny in its double lack of utility, and it is precisely through this humor and futility that the object comes closer to embodying its visceral paper-ness.

Zoe Nelson was born in Rhinebeck, New York, in 1983 and currently lives and works in Chicago, Illinois. She received an MFA from Columbia University in May, 2009. Zoe has exhibited at galleries in New York and Chicago, including Roots & Culture Contemporary Art Center (Chicago), Robert Bills Contemporary (Chicago), the Fisher Landau Center For Art (Long Island City), and NURTUREart (Williamsburg). In September 2012, Zoe is scheduled to have a solo exhibition at Lloyd Dobler Gallery, Chicago. Zoe's work was selected for the 2011 Midwest edition of *New American Paintings*, and she received the Ellen Battell Stoeckel Fellowship to attend Yale's Norfolk Summer Program in 2005.

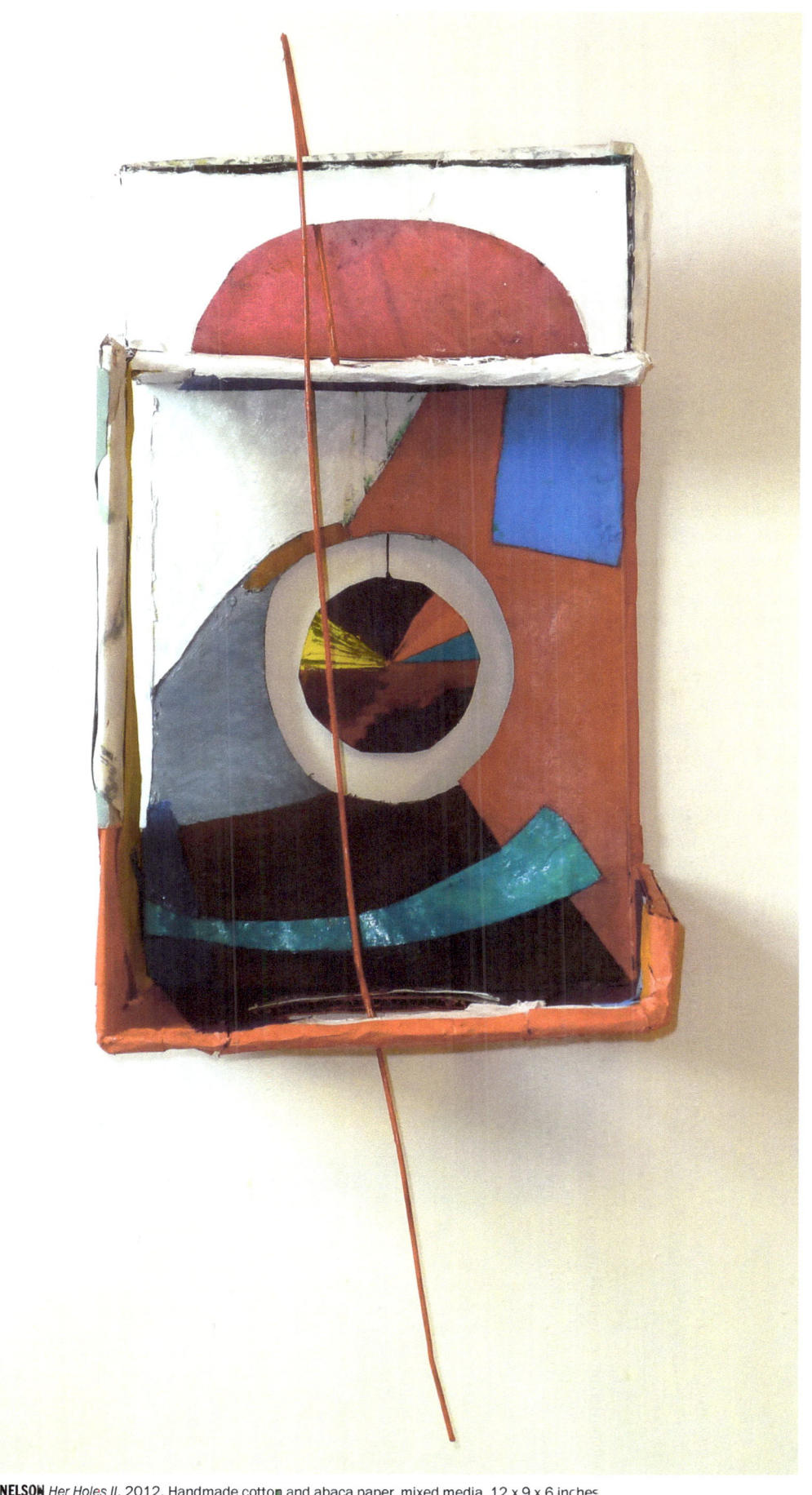

ZOE NELSON *Her Holes II*, 2012. Handmade cotton and abaca paper, mixed media. 12 x 9 x 6 inches.

IAN SCHNELLER

We often regard the utility of paper in a casual manner, perhaps only noticing it as we reach over to pull a freshly printed sheet out of our laser printer. In this context, paper serves merely as a ground, a substrate, or a platform for ink. We seldom regard the structural potential of paper, but when its interlocking fibers are infused with a vehicle like resin it creates a composite structure with a formidable strength.

The tradition of hand-pulling and pressing paper yields a medium that is particularly well-suited to resin infusion. It literally drinks up the vehicle because of its absorptive properties. The handmade paper provided to me for this project is so pure, white, and structurally profound that I have chosen to use it to create an incarnation of my audio horn speakers.

For years I have been making my horn speakers from recycled newsprint, baking soda, and dryer lint. This construction technique yields surfaces that are ruddy, organic, and wild like an untended garden. By contrast, the handmade paper horns are pristine, stripped down to the lines, and completely naked. Only hand-pulled paper can come close to this organic purity. It is similar to working with porcelain versus terra cotta or stoneware. Extra precaution is required when handling it during construction, but once impregnated it has amazing structural fortitude. In horn speaker construction, this is an absolute requirement for proper sonic performance.

The horn is an acoustic transformer that predates electronics and has existed in nature pre-dating man. Similarly, the process of papermaking is equally ancient. For me, the purity of the paper enhances the beauty and function of the horn's geometry, creating a uniquely organic symbiosis.

Ian Schneller, owner of Specimen Products, has been building custom guitars, tube amplifiers, and audio horn speakers for 25 years. Schneller began creating guitars while completing a master's degree from the School of the Art Institute of Chicago. His work soon expanded to include tube amplifiers and horn speakers.

In 2010, the *Sonic Arboretum*, a collaborative project between Schneller and composer/violinist Andrew Bird, debuted at New York's Guggenheim Museum. The *Sonic Arboretum* consists of a "forest" of horn speakers and tube amplifiers that Bird uses to create compositions for the exhibit. In 2011, the *Sonic Arboretum* exhibited at the Museum of Contemporary Art in Chicago for a month-long installation.

Schneller is also founder of the Chicago School of Guitar Making, where he teaches guitar and tube amplifier repair and building.

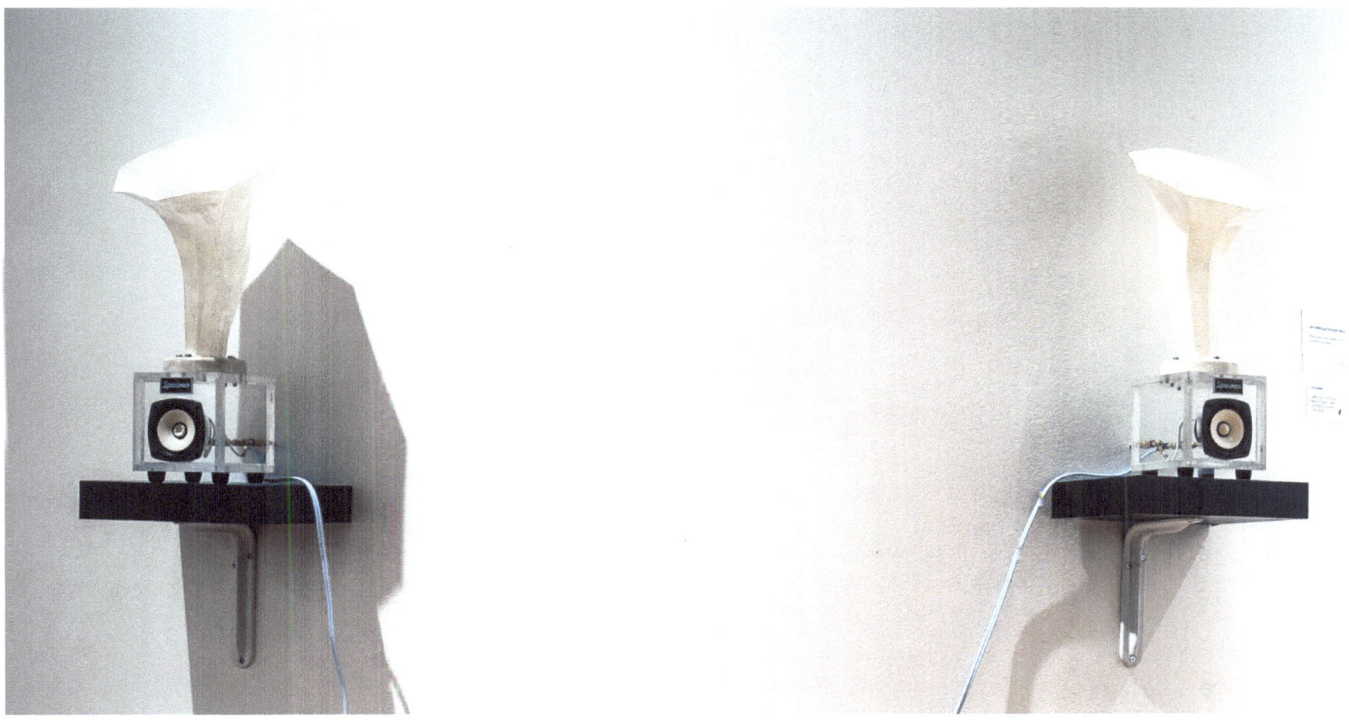

IAN SCHNELLER *White Hornlets*, 2012. Handmade cotton paper, mixed media. 19 x 19 x 5 inches.

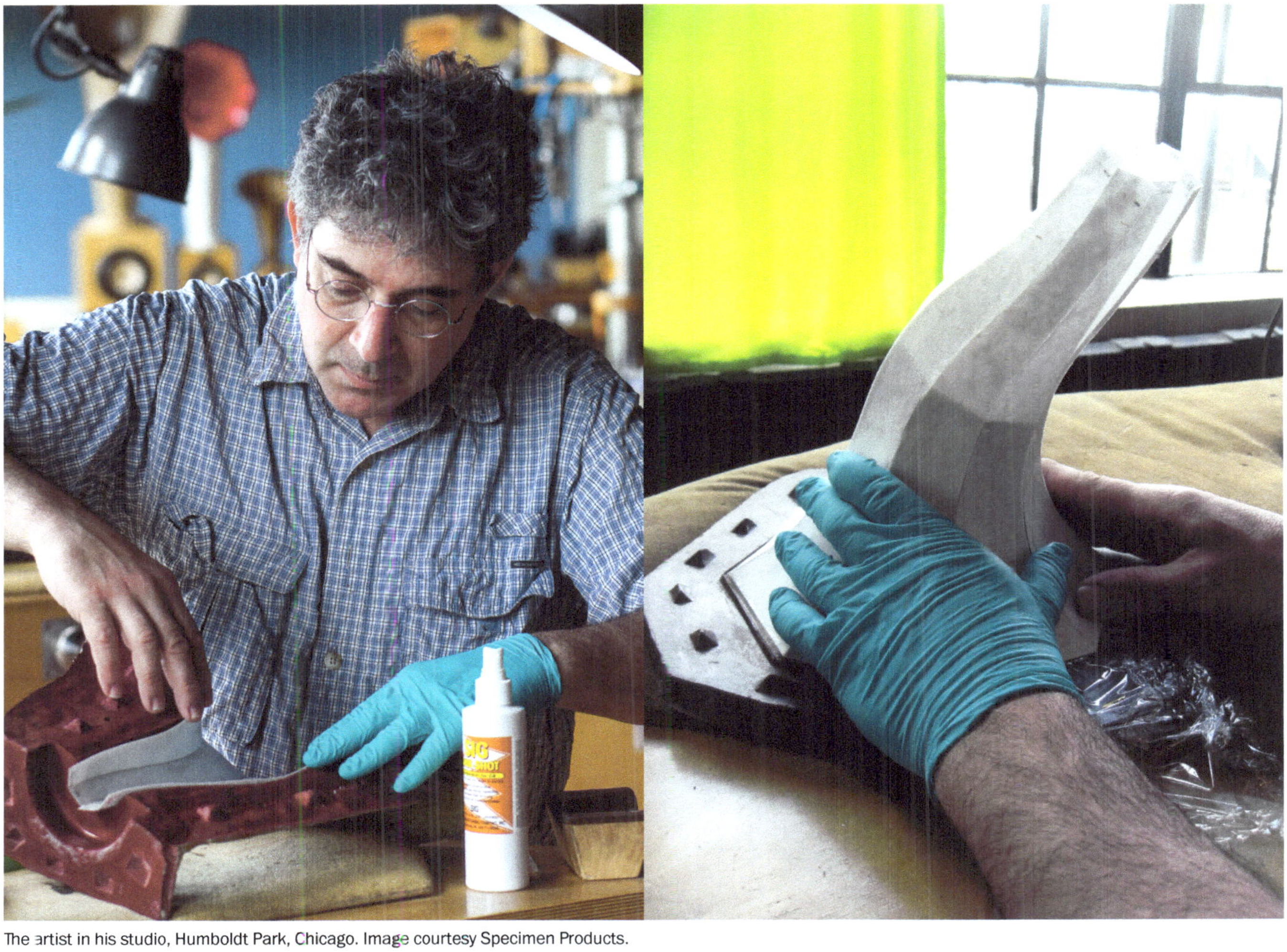

The artist in his studio, Humboldt Park, Chicago. Image courtesy Specimen Products.

DEBORAH BOARDMAN

Inflected by my recent trip to India and the vibrancy I experienced there, my project embraces both text and pattern. I wanted to respond intuitively to the idiosyncratic qualities of the paper fabricated for me by Hannah King. The cotton and abaca fibers hold gouache paint very differently, and I was challenged to remain nimble in my encounter with each sheet. I was especially fascinated by the transparency of the abaca, and the possibility of painting on each side of the sheet. I love its warm color and how the paint stays on its surface, unlike the more absorbent cotton sheets. The text paintings present a new direction, as earlier text works were contained inside larger projects like painted books. Here the text extends my practice of contemplative, fluid engagement with painting.

Deborah Boardman is a painter and installation artist and member of the Chicago-based artist collaborative ED JR. with Edra Soto, Jeroen Nelemans, and Ryan Richey. Recent projects include *Steady As She Goes*, a solo exhibition of paintings and site-specific wallpaper at EBERSMOORE gallery in Chicago; *Magic Mountain* in Bangalore, India; and *CoLaboratory* with ED JR. at Columbia College Chicago.

She received a BFA from Massachusetts College of Art (1984) and a MFA from Tufts University–School of the Museum of Fine Arts (1987). Deborah is a recipient of grants from the Illinois Arts Council and the Indiana Humanities Council. Her work is in the public collection of the Chicago Cultural Center, and her artist books are in collections of the Bibliothecha Alexandrina, Egypt; the Newberry's Wing Collection; and Harvard University's Houghton Library, among others.

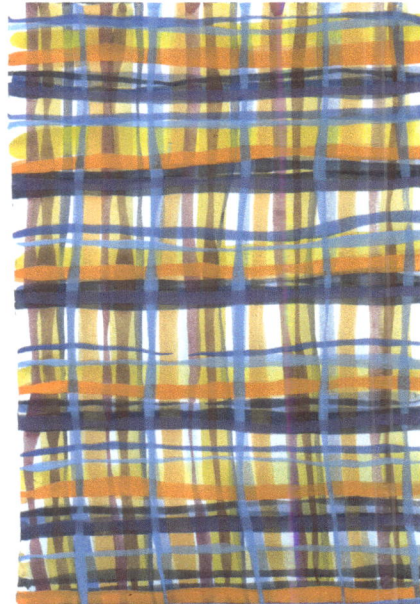

DEBORAH BOARDMAN *Notes to the Beloved and Other Remarks*, 2012. Gouache and mixed media on handmade cotton and abaca paper. Dimensions variable.

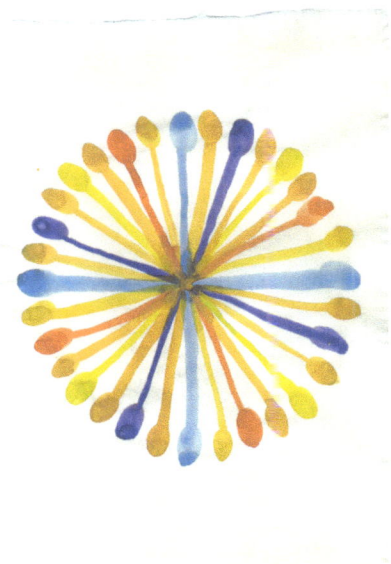

DEBORAH BOARDMAN *Notes to the Beloved and Other Remarks*, 2012. Gouache and mixed media on handmade cotton and abaca paper. Dimensions variable.

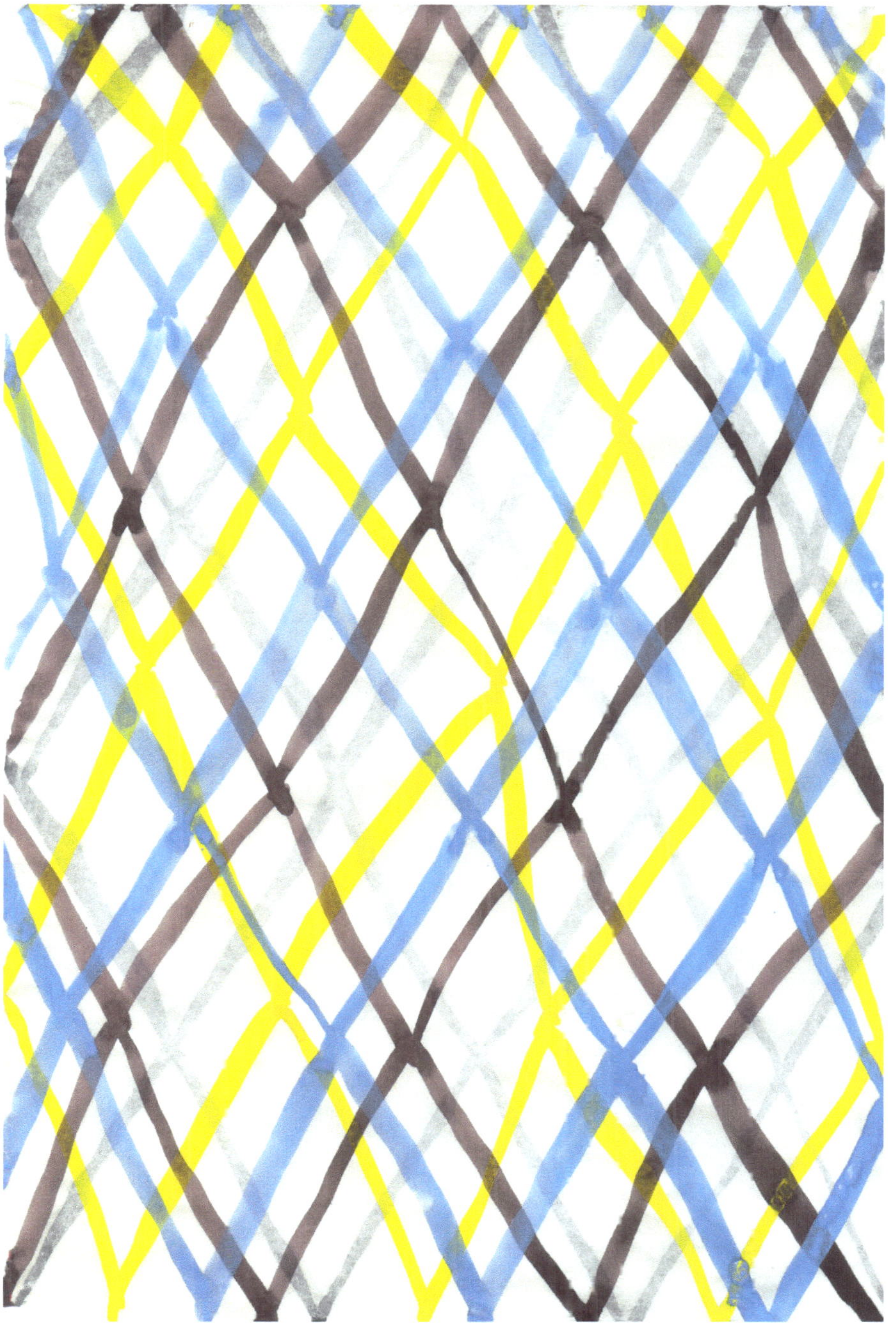

DEBORAH BOARDMAN *Notes to the Beloved and Other Remarks*, 2012. Gouache and mixed media on handmade cotton and abaca paper. Dimensions variable.

MATTHEW SHLIAN

As a paper engineer, my work is rooted in print media, book arts, and commercial design. Beginning with an initial fold, a single action causes a transfer of energy to subsequent folds, which ultimately manifest in drawings and three-dimensional forms. I use my engineering skills to create kinetic sculpture, which has lead to collaborations with scientists at the University of Michigan. Researchers see paper engineering as a metaphor for scientific principals; I see their inquiry as basis for artistic inspiration. In my studio I am a collaborator, explorer, and inventor. I begin with a system of folding and at a particular moment the material takes over. Guided by wonder, my work is made because I cannot visualize its final realization; in this way I come to understanding through curiosity.

Matthew Shlian is an artist, paper engineer, teacher, and collaborator. After graduating from Alfred University in 2002, Matthew spent three years working as a paper engineer in the field of commercial design. There he made movable paper contraptions, from popup books to greeting cards to artist books and kinetic sculptures. In 2006 he received his MFA from Cranbrook Academy of Art. Currently, he operates a design studio in Ann Arbor, Michigan; teaches Foundations and Paper Engineering at the University of Michigan; and works as a visiting research scholar in the university's Materials Science and Engineering department. His work can be seen at www.mattshlian.com.

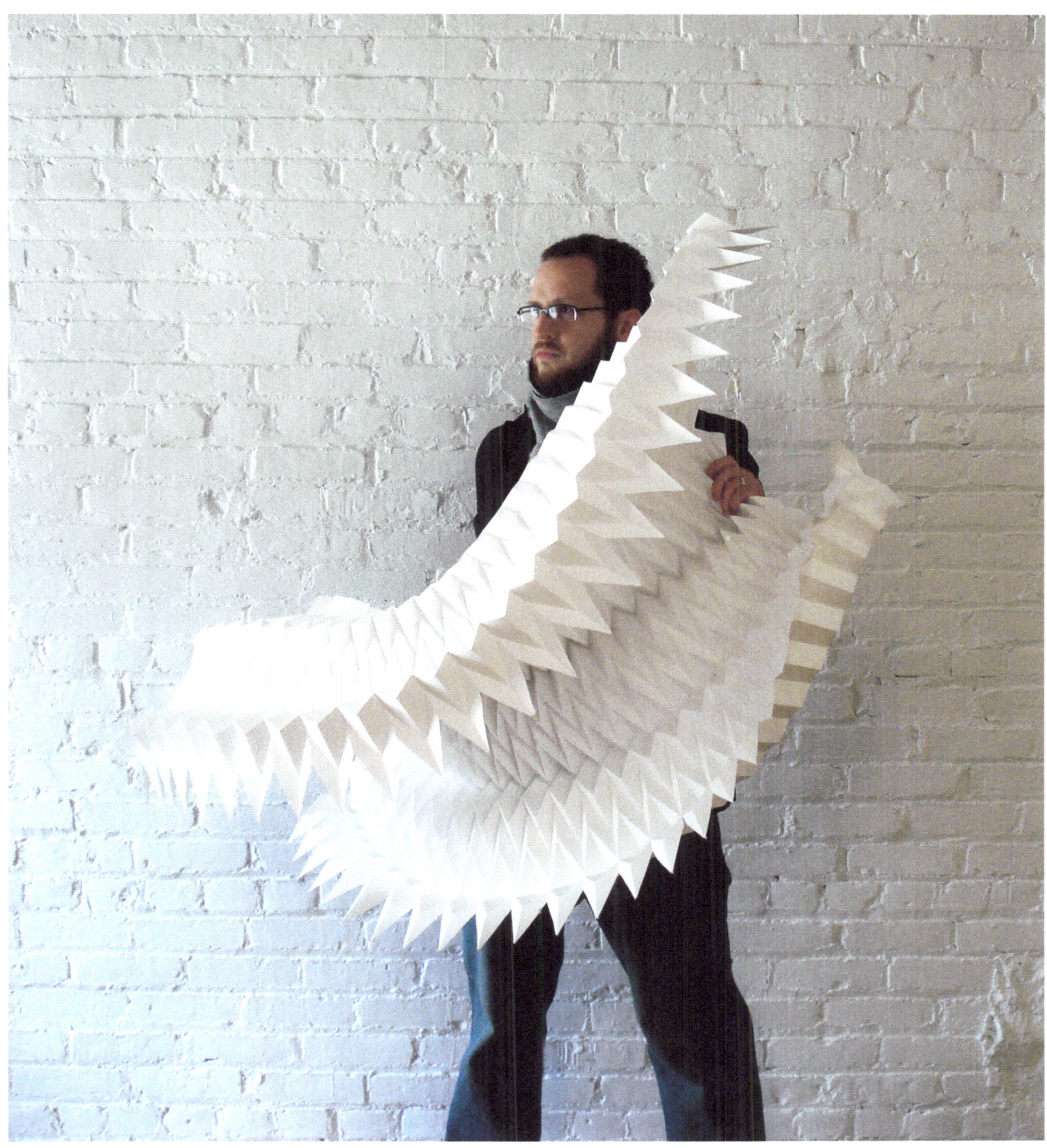

MATTHEW SHLIAN, *Pleat Study*, 2012. Handmade cotton paper. Dimensions variable.

DANIEL LUEDTKE

By mutating and reprocessing found footage, drawings, photographs, and narratives I create representational imagery that flirts with abstraction, rehabilitating queer, feminist, and personal subject matter through and alongside non-representational forms such as patterning and geometric formalism. Montaged images from the '60s and '70s Women's Movement, re-drawn gay clichés, and references to HIV/AIDS are reframed to evoke new possibilities of framing queer history and memory. Slippery objects and figures cause a tension in the viewing process as the specificity of the subject matter is both acknowledged and subverted. These images and processes create an androgynous aesthetic that replicates my desires for concrete communities devoid of totalizing essentialism.

For *Material Assumptions*, I was interested in creating a framework for collaboration with the papermakers and curators of the exhibition. Instead of planning a specific work and dictating the materials required for its creation, I wanted to use the creation of the raw materials as an excuse or reason to create a dialog surrounding the traditionally feminized craft of paper. I asked the papermakers to craft materials of their choice and to include their own instructions, intentions and ideas for its use. With this paper acting as a contract or trusting pact, I have taken these instructions in mind as I fabricate each piece, keeping the desires and intentions of my collaborators intact throughout the process.

Daniel Luedtke is an artist, musician, and community organizer working in various mediums such as printmaking, video, sound, and writing. Luedtke got his start as a self-taught printmaker making silk-screened posters and record packaging for various music-related projects. He was awarded a Jerome Residency at Highpoint Center for Printmaking in 2008, has exhibited work in solo and group shows in the United States and abroad, and has been published in print anthologies for Princeton Architectural Press and Chronicle Books. In 2011, Luedtke helped co-found Madame, a community art center in Minneapolis, Minnesota, and is currently an MFA candidate at the School of the Art Institute of Chicago.

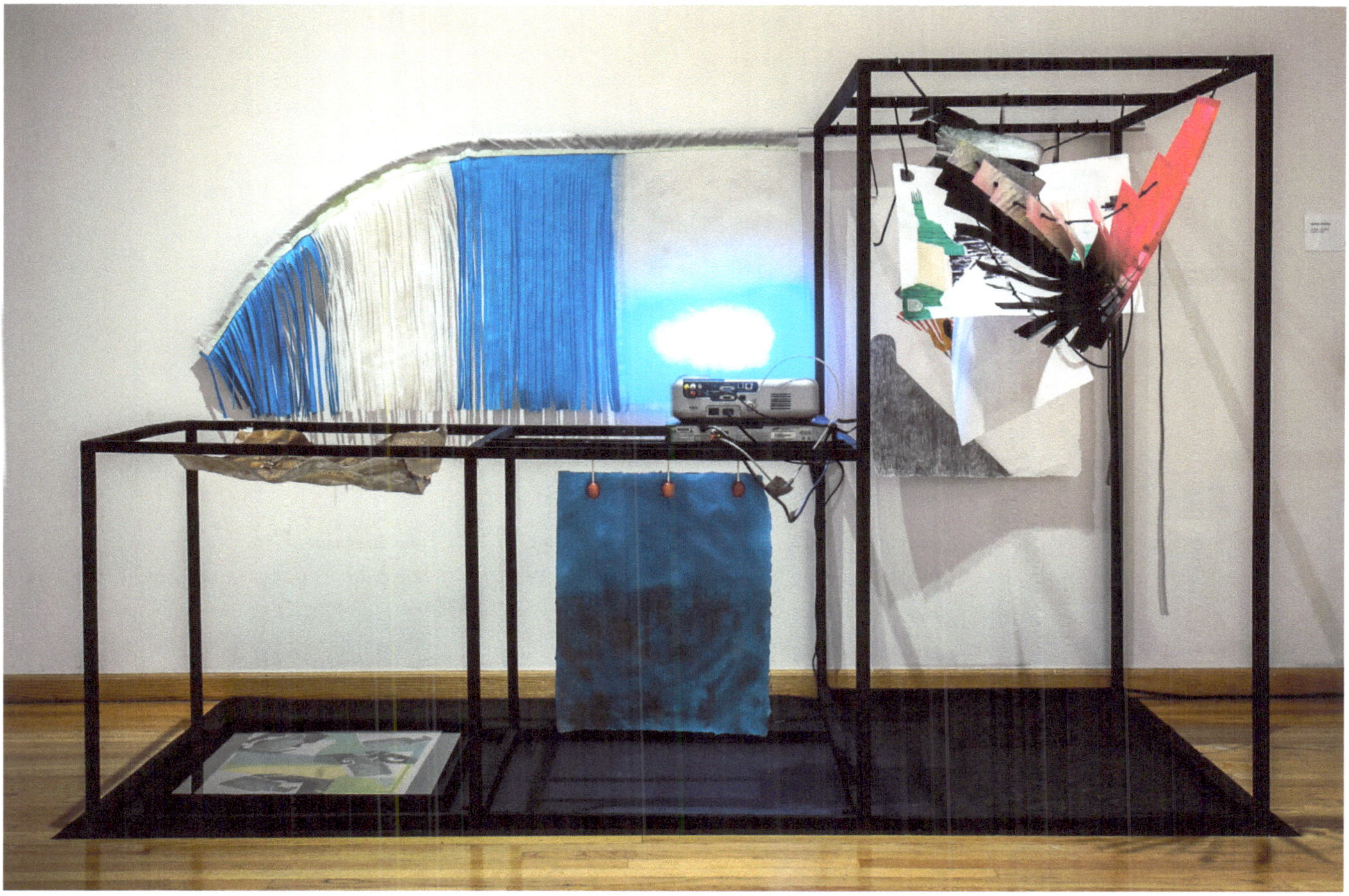

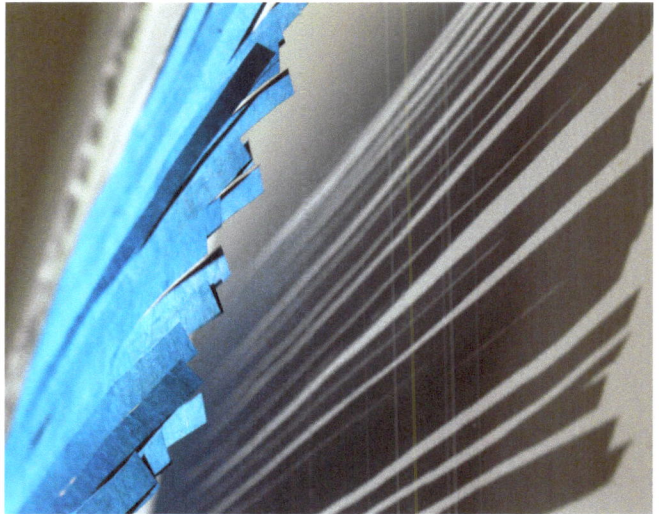

DANIEL LUEDTKE *Birthday Girl*, 2012. Mixed media installation. Dimensions variable.

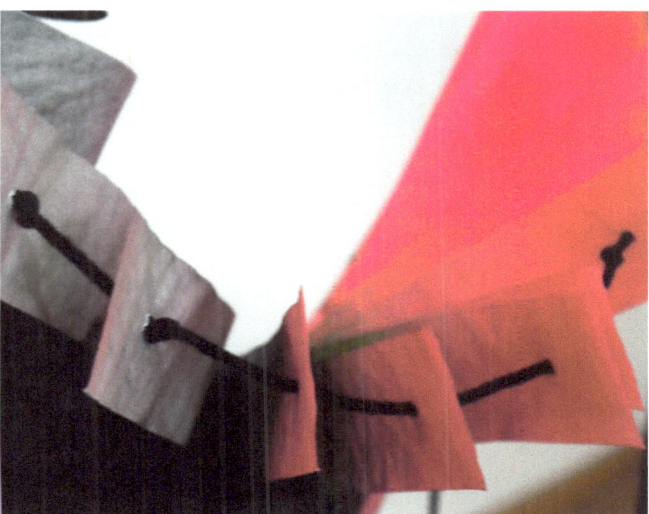

DANIEL LUEDTKE *Birthday Girl*, 2012 (detail). Handmade cotton paper.

DANIEL LUEDTKE *Birthday Girl*, 2012 (detail). Handmade cotton paper.

ANNICA CUPPETELLI
& CRISTOBAL MENDOZA

Our work normally sits in the space between the virtual and the real, but the invitation to participate in *Material Assumptions* gave us an opportunity to explore the relationship between real and virtual, physical and digital, even further. Our piece relies on a technique that we have been developing for almost two years: an interactive projection of lines is cast on a structure or physical object that acts to create an interference (moiré) pattern, which itself is a manifestation of a different kind of "in-between." Given that we would be provided with handmade paper as a material for the piece, we thought it would be interesting to involve it in our "traditional" process, as well as to extend this process by applying an additional layer of mechanization and digitization to both the design and the fabrication of the work. On the design side, the pattern that was cut into the paper was created using a simple program that generated rectangles whose widths were altered using a sinusoidal function. Thus, the design is not the outcome of drafting (or even "mousing"); rather, it is the result of a numerical expression. The fabrication was made by using a laser cutter, itself a machine controlled by numerical expressions. We thought it interesting then to have this beautifully imperfect handmade paper be altered via processes that begin in the purely abstract and perfect world of numbers, but have a manifestation in the physical world via digital technologies. Again, given that our work tends to live in the "in-between" of the virtual and the real, transforming the handmade via digital/automated processes felt like yet another "in-between" that our work is now able to occupy.

Annica Cuppetelli (United States) and **Cristobal Mendoza** (Venezuela) began their artistic collaboration in the fall of 2010. Their work has been exhibited in the Biennial of Video and New Media Art, Chile, 2012; and festivals such as FILE 2011 and FAD 2011 Brazil; and video_dumbo 2011, New York; among others. Cuppetelli obtained her MFA from Cranbrook Academy of Art (Fiber, 2008) and Mendoza at the Rhode Island School of Design (Digital Media, 2007). Mendoza is an assistant professor at Wayne State University in Detroit, Michigan.

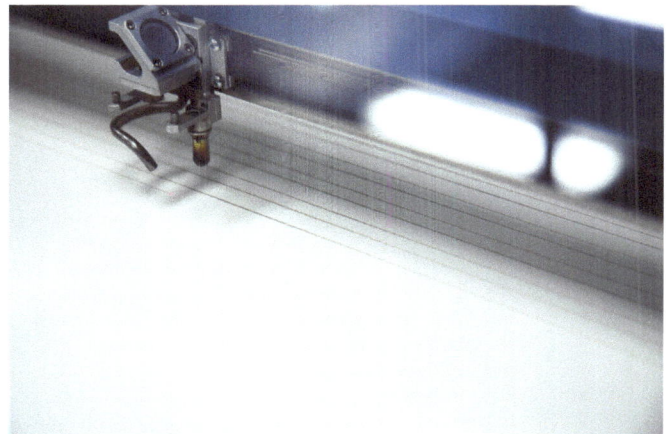

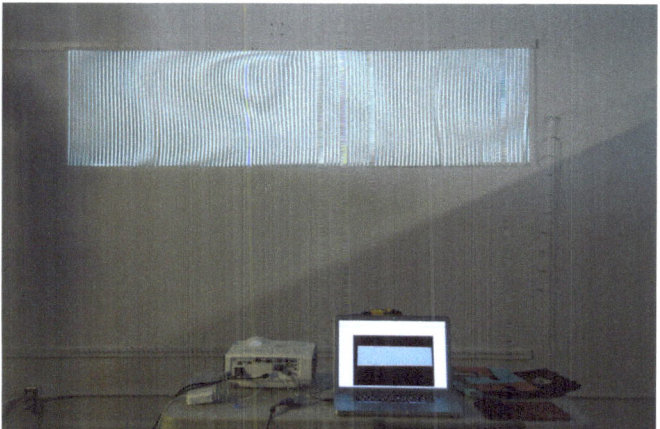

ANNICA CUPPETELLI & CRISTOBAL MENDOZA *Double Interference*, 2012 (in progress).

ANNICA CUPPETELLI & CRISTOBAL MENDOZA *Double Interference*, 2012 (in progress).

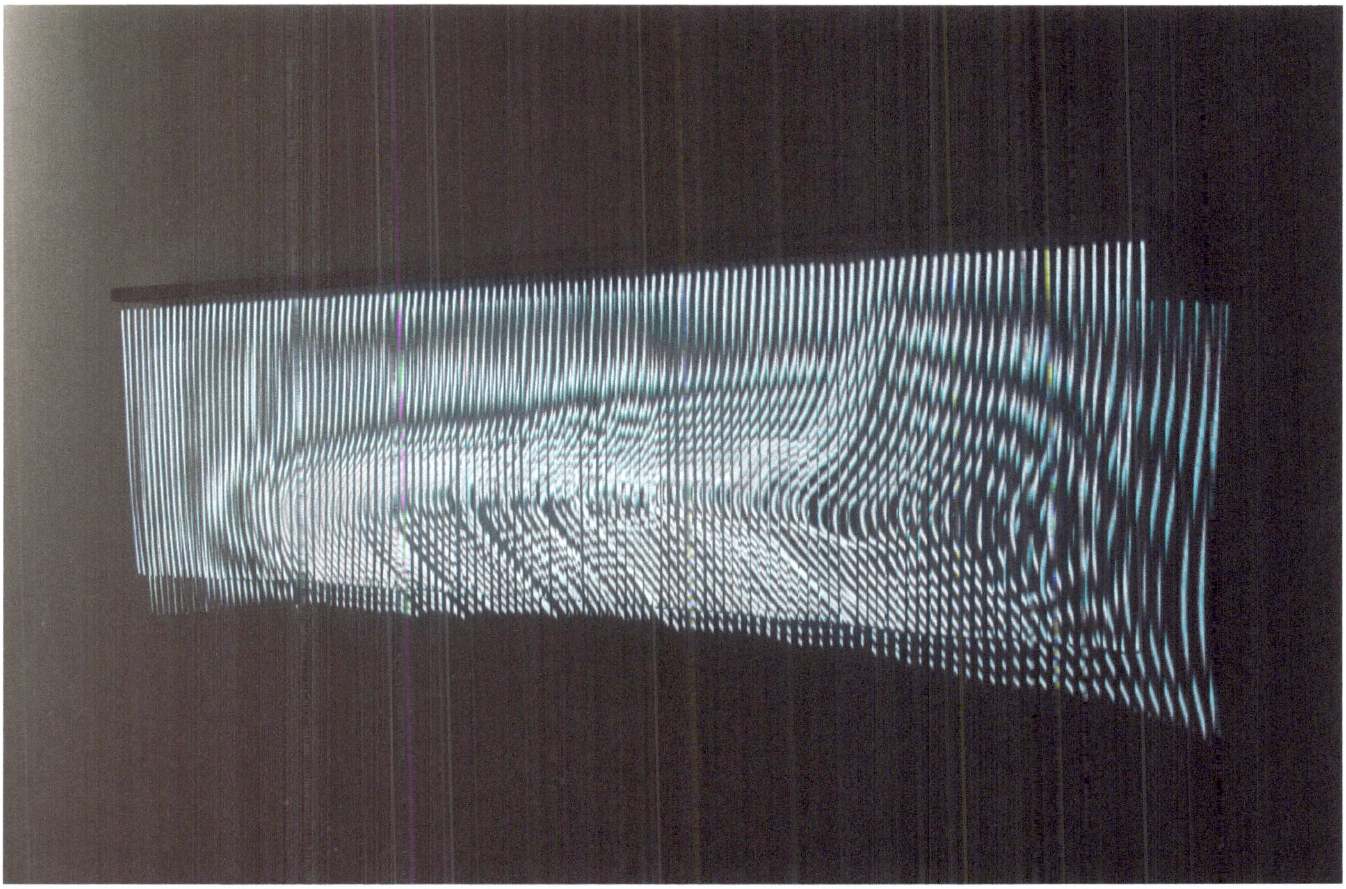

ANNICA CUPPETELLI & CRISTOBAL MENDOZA *Double Interference*, 2012. Handmade cotton paper, MDF, computer, video projector, camera, custom software. Dimensions variable.

DAN DEVENING

My contribution to the *Material Assumptions* exhibition reflects a long-running relationship with paper as a material to work upon and as well as to work through. For years, I've been deconstructing the paper I use for a drawing in order to break down the picture plane to build some new kind of structural assemblies. The beautiful paper provided by the Center for Book and Paper Arts became a very special opportunity for the ways in which I work with paper. As I begin a piece, the compositional elements—images, shapes, lines, etc.—are drawn on and then cut away from the paper. These pieces are then activated with pigment or drawing and then repositioned back to their respective places to reclaim the full plane. Using inlay to put everything back together, the cut edge becomes an important part of the form. The edge suggests a kind of certainty that is never fulfilled by the full composition. I then build up the final image with collaged elements; the collage acts as a kind of "repair" for those parts of the composition that require structural support or enhancement. The compositions are always based on the small, quickly made drawings that fill my sketchbooks; the drawings often suggest wonky, non-functional architecture. I'm drawn to inadequately built forms, especially those that fail, are hobbled together, ridiculously embellished, buttressed to keep from falling, or simply can't live up to their own potential. As a reflection of the human spirit, these structures suggest an inspiring kind of optimism.

Dan Devening is an artist, educator, and curator living in Chicago. He is currently adjunct professor in the Department of Painting and Drawing at the School of the Art Institute of Chicago. In the United States his work has been featured at the Roy Boyd Gallery, the Chicago Cultural Center, Terra Museum of American Art, EBERSMOORE gallery, and Julius Caesar in Chicago; Kinkead Contemporary in Los Angeles; and Printed Matter, Inc. in New York. Other projects include international exhibitions at the Kunstverein Recklinghausen, Museum Kurhaus in Kleve, galerie oqbo, and Renate Schroeder Gallery in Germany; Art Metropole in Toronto; De Appel in Amsterdam; Secession in Vienna; and Galerie des Multiples in Paris. In 2007 he inaugurated, and currently directs, devening projects + editions, a gallery project featuring exhibitions and site-specific installations by emerging and established international artists.

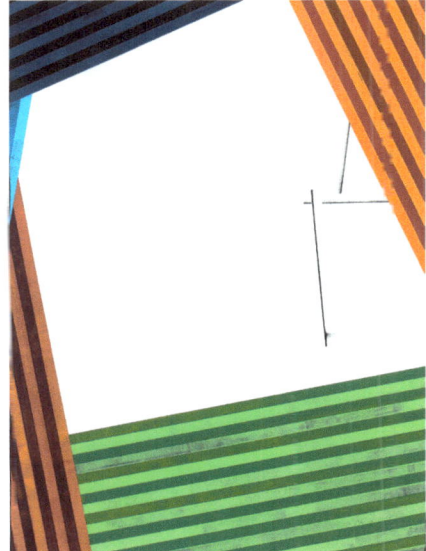

DAN DEVENING *Untitled*, 2012. Acrylic and collage on handmade cotton paper. 30 x 32 inches.

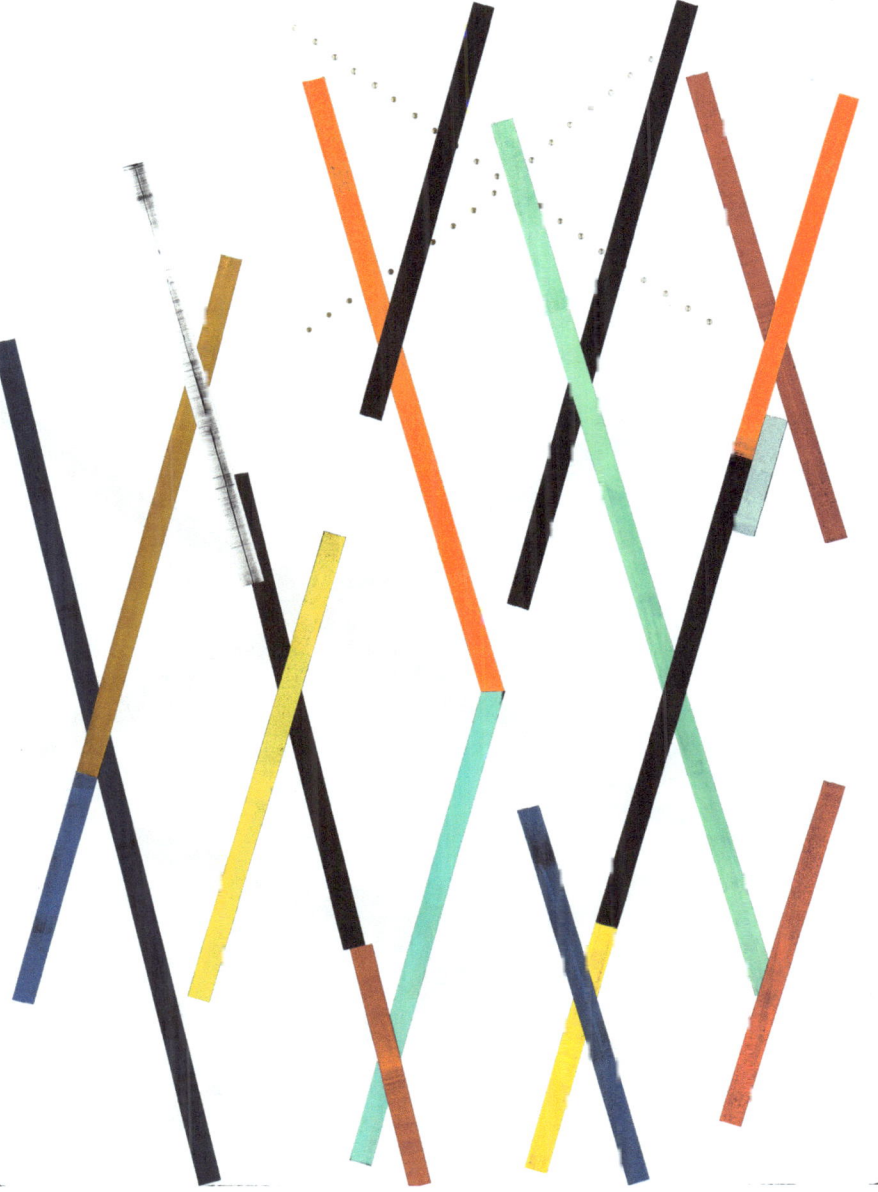

DAN DEVENING *Untitled*, 2012. Acrylic and collage on handmade cotton paper. 30 x 32 inches.

KATE MCQUILLEN

For the past year, I've been making works about the disparity between makeshift weapons and the sophisticated tools of the US military. Recently, I've become somewhat paranoid about this project. This past summer, for instance, I made a series of tiny sculptures. Using everyday objects and household materials, I wound together a bunch of tiny fake IEDs. When I searched for images to base the work on, I typed the phrase "improvised explosive devices" into a search engine. I cringed, and thought to myself, "How many times can one google that phrase before Homeland Security comes knocking on your door?" As it turns out, I was not being completely paranoid. When these works were shipped across the border to a show in Canada, the art handlers refused to take them until they were "disassembled."

After a studio visit a few months ago, concerned patrons suggested that I register with the police before continuing on with this work. Then in the winter, I started on a project about exploded pipe bombs, made from clay. I went to Home Depot to buy a pipe to use for a mold. When I asked for help finding the right size cap, the employee paused, looked at my six-inch lead pipe and asked, "You aren't making a pipe bomb, are ya, lady?" I was speechless, and ran through the possible answers in my head, one of which, frighteningly, could have been a form of "yes." I very quickly said no, ran to the register, and made sure to pay in cash.

Though my interest in this comes purely from what I've observed in the past few years as a trend of suspicion invading everyday life, I've also started to feel some type of odd guilt in making these works. It's not unlike the feeling I get when I go through security at the airport, where even though I know I have no weapons or anything to hide, I'm still afraid of getting caught.

The project for *Material Assumptions* addresses my fears of being suspected as a terrorist by, in a way, embracing them. I've taken my own clothes and sewn faked weapons into the pockets, then ran them through the printing press to transfer the image onto paper. The result is images that look like x-rays picking up traces of weapons. There is an absurdity to the works that matches the absurdity of my fears of being suspected as a terrorist; the "weapons" are either benign materials like large quantities of matches, or they are in clear view, as through a pair of pantyhose.

There is an implication in this work that we are all, for the instant that we pass through security screenings, viewed as potential terrorists no matter who we may be. They depict only the clothes and the weapons, leaving out the form of the body itself. There is a sense, however, through the folds of the fabrics that someone, or more to the point anyone, could be inside them.

Kate McQuillen is a Chicago-based artist working in print, installation, and sculpture. She is currently serving as the printmaking artist-in-residence at Lillstreet Art Center in Chicago, and as director of the Chicago Printers Guild. McQuillen has attended residencies in Europe and Canada, and is represented in Canada by O'Born Contemporary. Her work examines makeshift weaponry, the destructive power inherent in seemingly mundane objects, and the American public's relationship to surveillance and security in the wake of the terrorist attacks of the past decade.

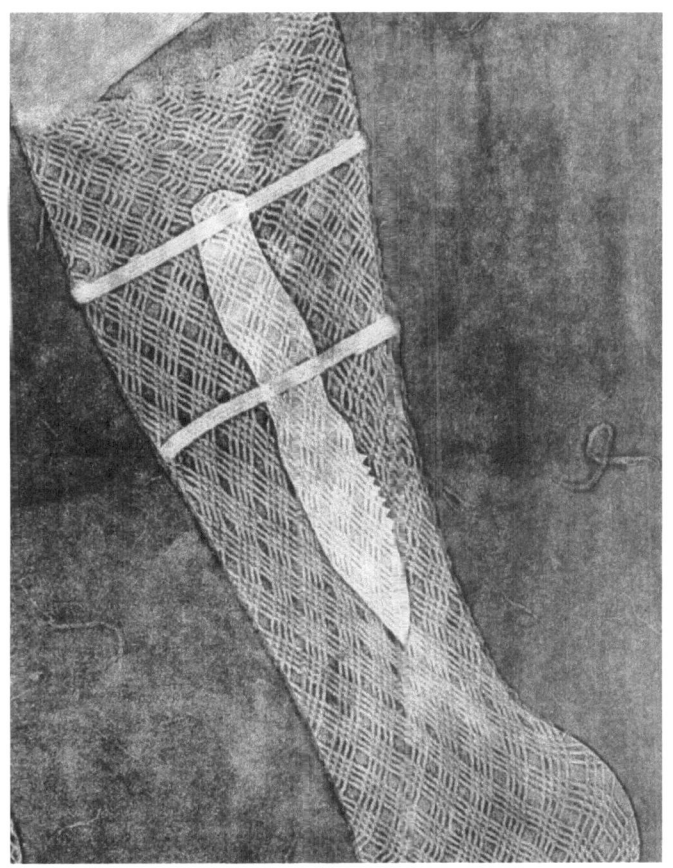

KATE MCQUILLEN *Hose*, 2012. Pressure monoprint on abaca handmade paper. 22 x 30 inches.

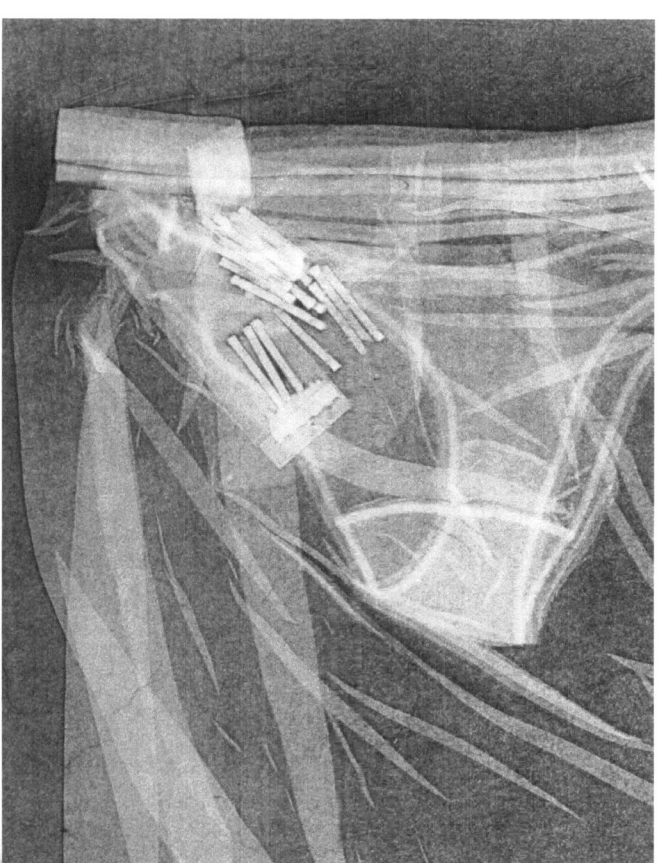

KATE MCQUILLEN *Skirt*, 2012. Pressure monoprint on cotton handmade paper. 22 x 30 inches.

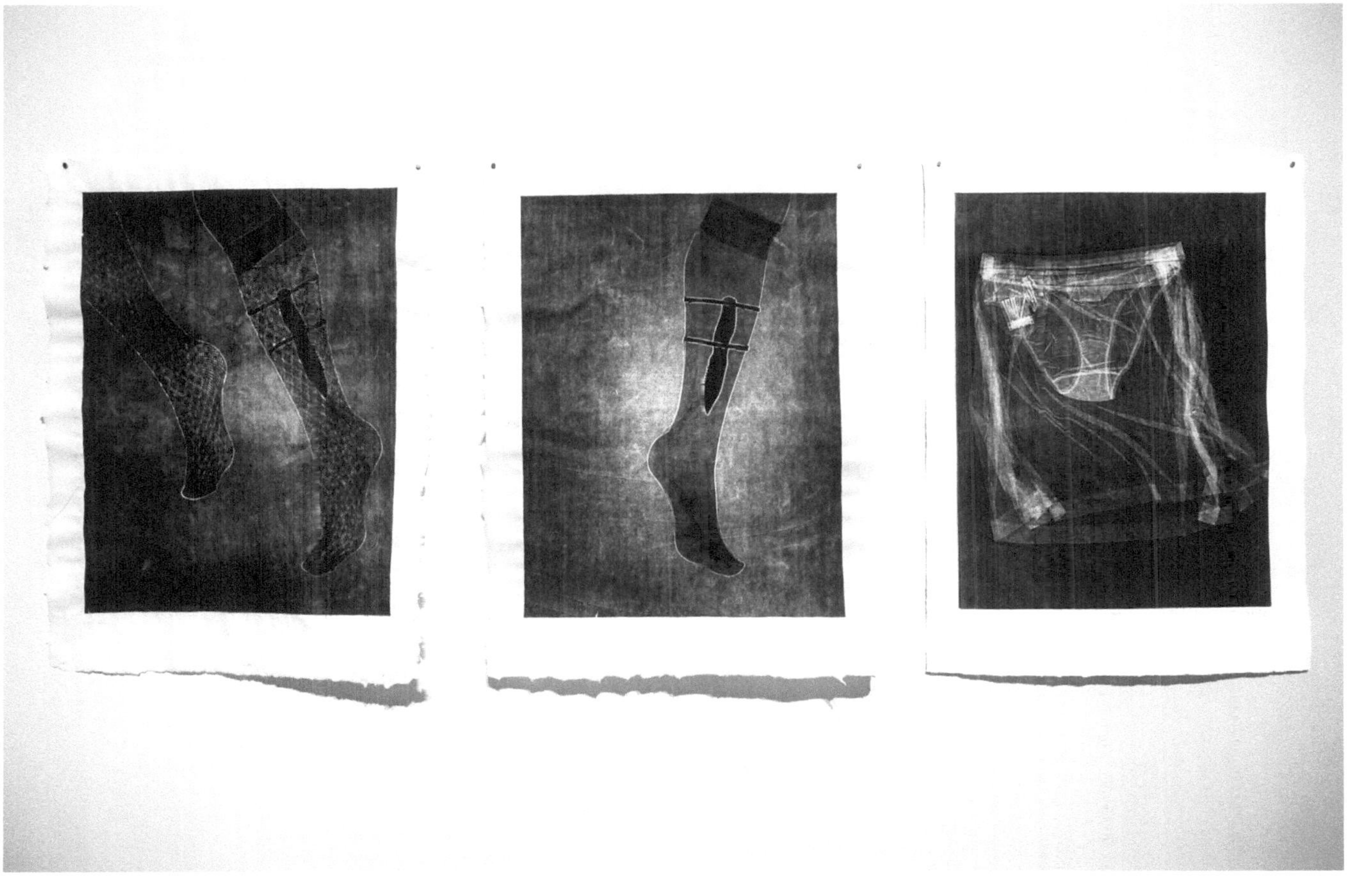

KATE MCQUILLEN Installation view.

JULIE SCHENKELBERG

My practice is centered on the interior psychology of the home and the objects of everyday life. My work displays the confinement and accumulation of oppressive social norms, until it visibly hits a breaking point. The objects I sculpt—everyday functional objects—become dysfunctional as I alter them into the destruction and dysfunction they have collected over time. I seek to display hidden confinement through opening up and dissecting objects, showing the hidden dysfunction of relationships in these spaces. I illuminate social confinement through the physical combustion of my sculptural objects.

Julie Schenkelberg currently lives and works in Brooklyn, New York. She was born in Cleveland, Ohio, in 1974. She currently shows at Asya Geisberg Gallery in New York. Julie attended the MFA fine arts program at the School of Visual Arts, New York, in 2011, and holds a BA in Art History from the College of Wooster, Ohio. Her large-scale sculptural installations are a result of 15 years of working in scenic theater painting shops around the country.

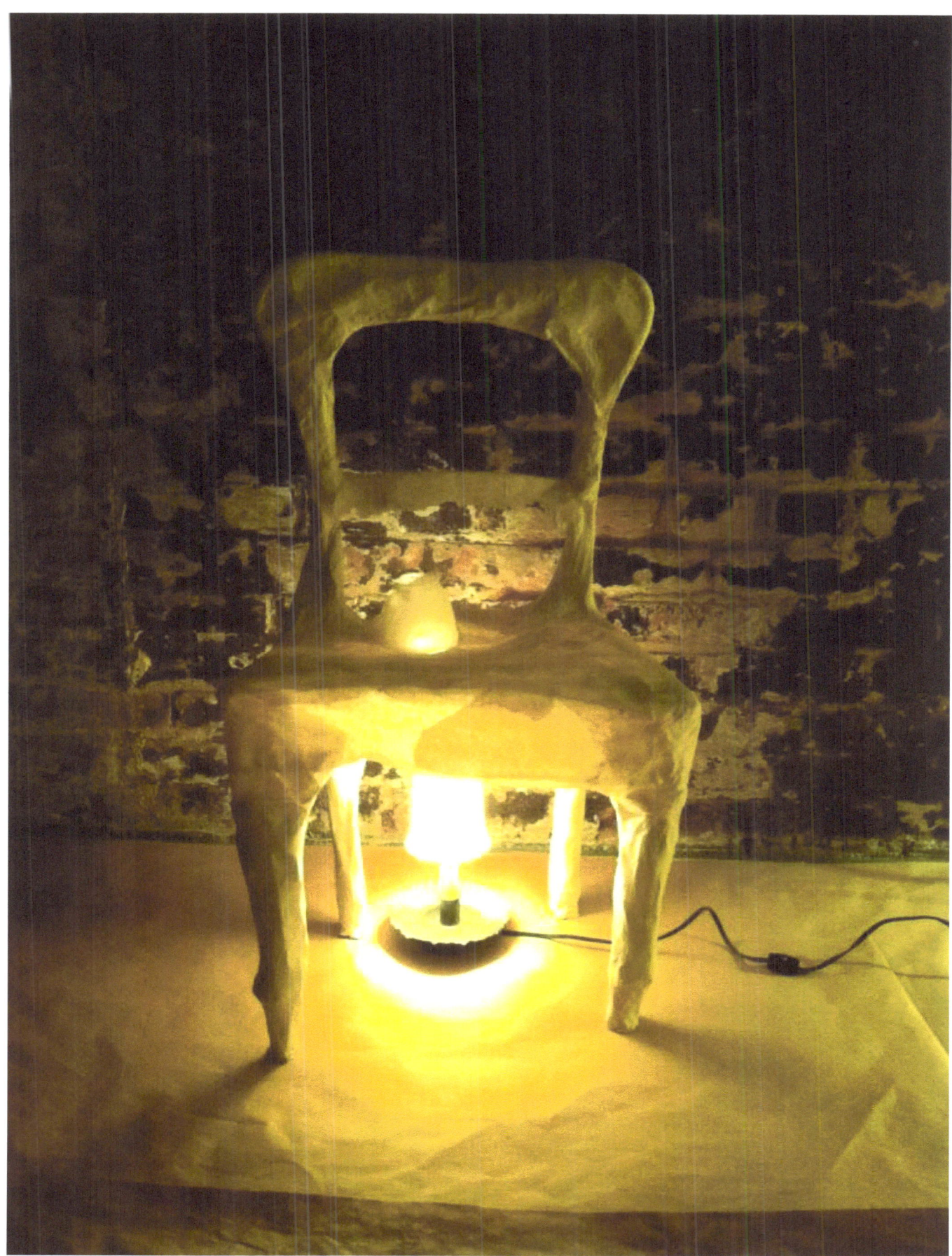

JULIE SCHENKELBERG *Echo*, 2012. Abaca handmade paper, glue, and lamp with handmade shade. 17 x 14 x 30 inches.

ANNA TSANTIR

My work has to do with the tension I find between the common and the unique. Representations of commonplace subject matter are many times tragic or sexual. Often I use animal imagery to represent innocents at the mercy of human ideologies such as providence or the way we behave as stewards of our environment. I also work with abstracted sexual and geometric imagery and patterning concerning nature and the basic elements.

Formally, I explore various simple processes that become a meditation on the content. The intent is that my process takes what is real and specific into the realm of the universal or metaphysical. This includes repeating an image or a motion so that the action of making the piece becomes contemplative. Repeated imagery and patterns are the same, yet different, and they reflect biological events and patterns found in nature. I also use light and shadow so the line between what is "real" and what is perceived about reality becomes ambiguous and the viewer questions the source of the image.

I utilize weaving, paper cutting, sewing, bookmaking, tracing, printing, and copying to meditate on the powerful visual and the emotive impact of the repeated image. And the idea that these mediums are neglected, or considered the "lesser" or secondary arts, and in many cases the feminine arts, is very much of interest to me.

Anna Tsantir works and lives in Minneapolis, Minnesota. After completing her BA in Art History at the University of Minnesota, she began to learn printmaking while living in Wyoming. She then received her MFA from the Memphis College of Art, where she first started to combine print, book, and sculpture. Tsantir has exhibited work nationally and internationally. Highlights include: a solo exhibition at Second Floor Contemporary in Memphis; *Artists and the Art of the Book*, a traveling exhibition curated by the Experimental Print Institute in Pennsylvania; *Labor/Leisure* in the Common Room at the Soap Factory in Minneapolis; and *Anguish* at the MCA Center Gallery in Memphis. Tsantir is the recipient of a Forecast Public Art Jerome Planning Grant in 2011, a Minnesota State Arts Board Artist Initiative Grant in 2009, and the Jerome Emerging Printmakers Residency at Highpoint Center for Printmaking in 2009. Currently, Tsantir works from her studio in Minneapolis and is one of the founding members of the bookmaking collaborative, Adult Books.

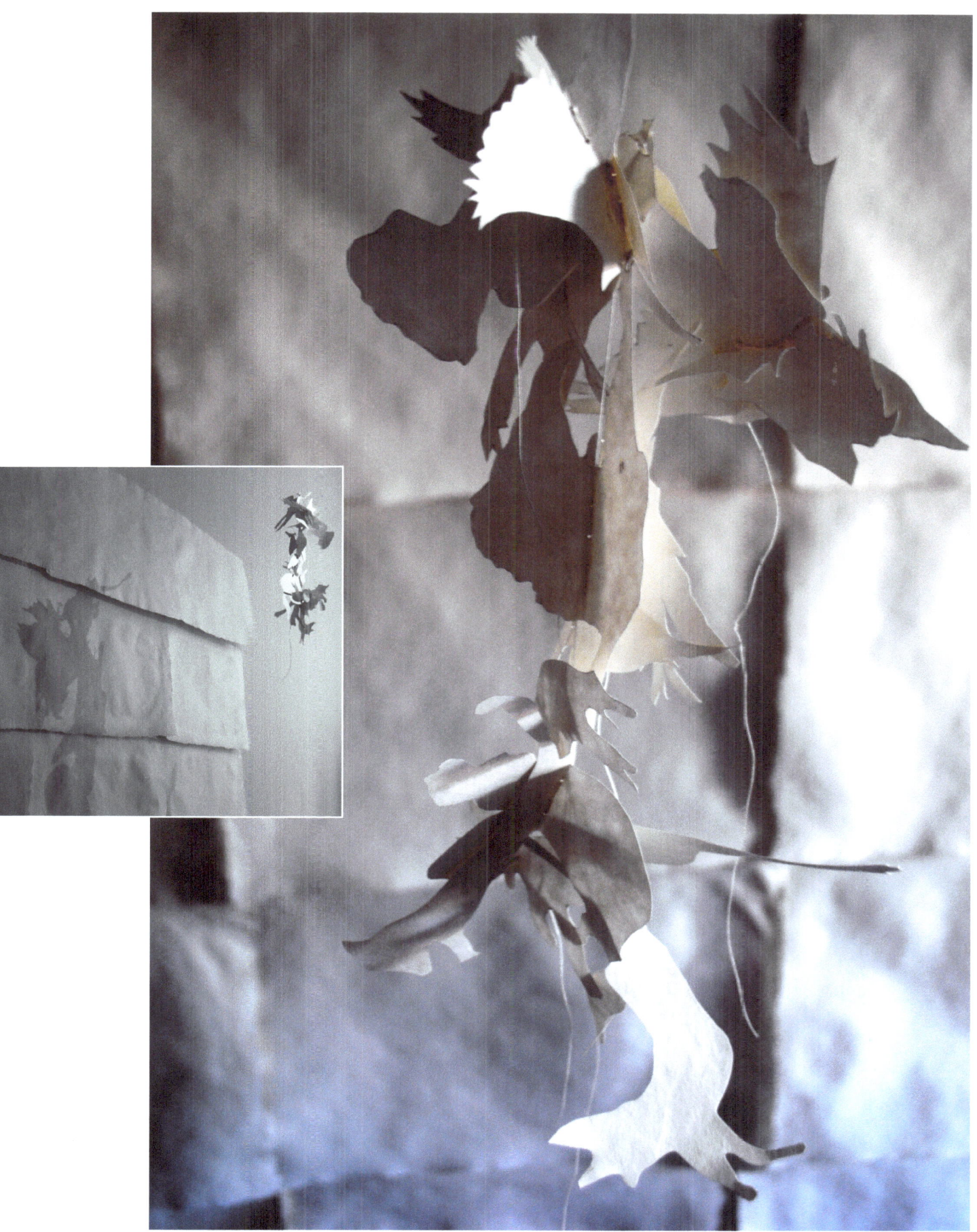

ANNA TSANTIR *The Raven and the Wolf* (detail), 2012. Handmade abaca paper, string.

NIALL MCCLELLAND

I treated the paper provided to me to various states of decay through placing deteriorating metal objects, found through scouring my industrial neighborhood, on top of the paper for a period of time, then printed traces of these objects on the paper to see how the paper would react to the forms of the objects and the rust covering them. Taking some of the work outside of the studio to let the weather assist in the process through sun bleaching, burial, stapling to poles, etc., helped to contrast some of the more controlled pieces worked on within my studio. I attemped to integrate the paper into my neighborhood and leave its traces on the work, giving the pieces a semblance of the found paper I collect through my daily walks on the train tracks adjacent to my studio, whether it's the cardboard boxes mutated over the course of a harsh winter, or the gig posters bleached by the intense summer sun and stretched by rainstorms. The finished paper is transformed by my interventions and the natural wear and tear of the elements into an honest reflection of my surroundings.

Niall McClelland (b.1980) lives and works in Toronto and went to school in Vancouver. He has recently had solo shows at Clint Roenisch Gallery, Toronto, and Eleanor Harwood Gallery, San Francisco, and has been included in group shows at PPOW, New York, and the Museum of Contemporary Canadian Art, Toronto. With work rooted in drawing and basic mark making, using folded photocopies, old bed-sheets, fragile newsprint, spray paint, and other basic materials, McClelland makes compelling works that radiate a sense of formal elegance with arte povera-like zeal and (a little bit of) the sneering contrariness born of punk music. He has recently been published in *Modern Painters*, *Canadian Art*, and *Bad Day* magazine.

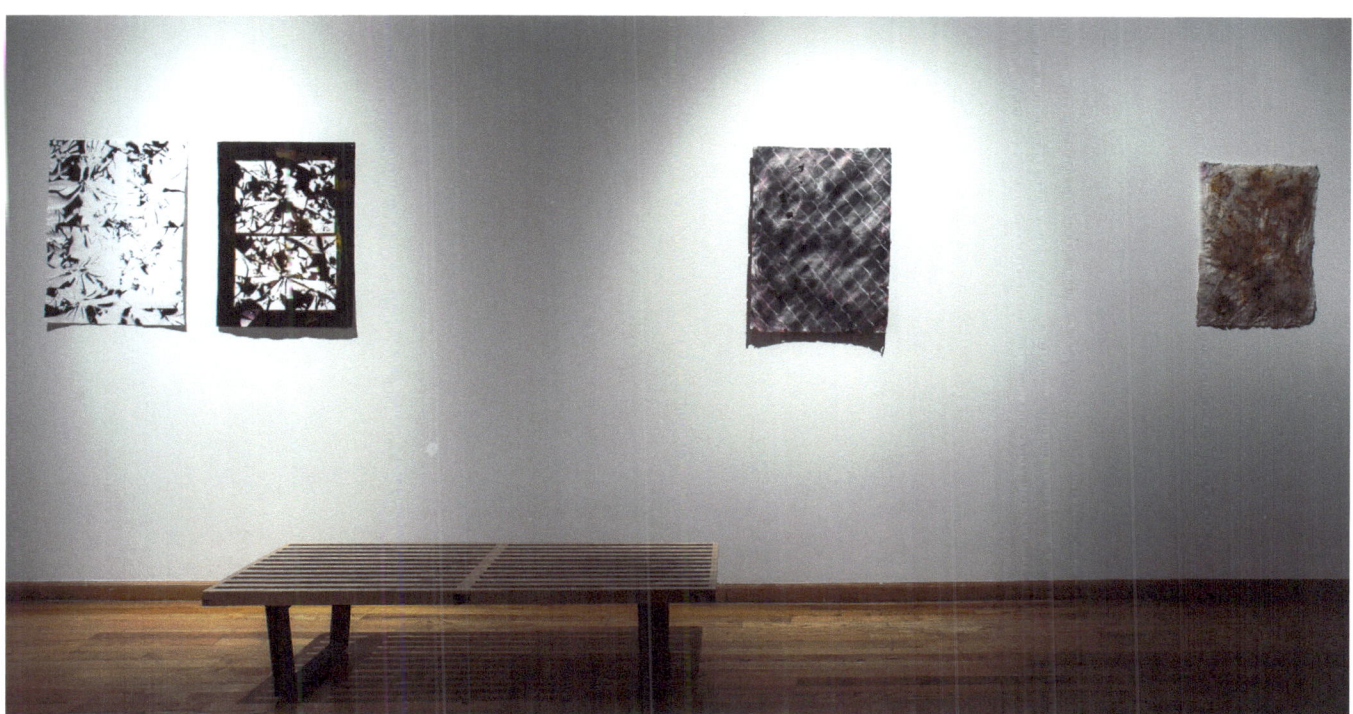

NIALL MCCLELLAND *Traces 1–4*, 2012. Mixed media on cotton paper.

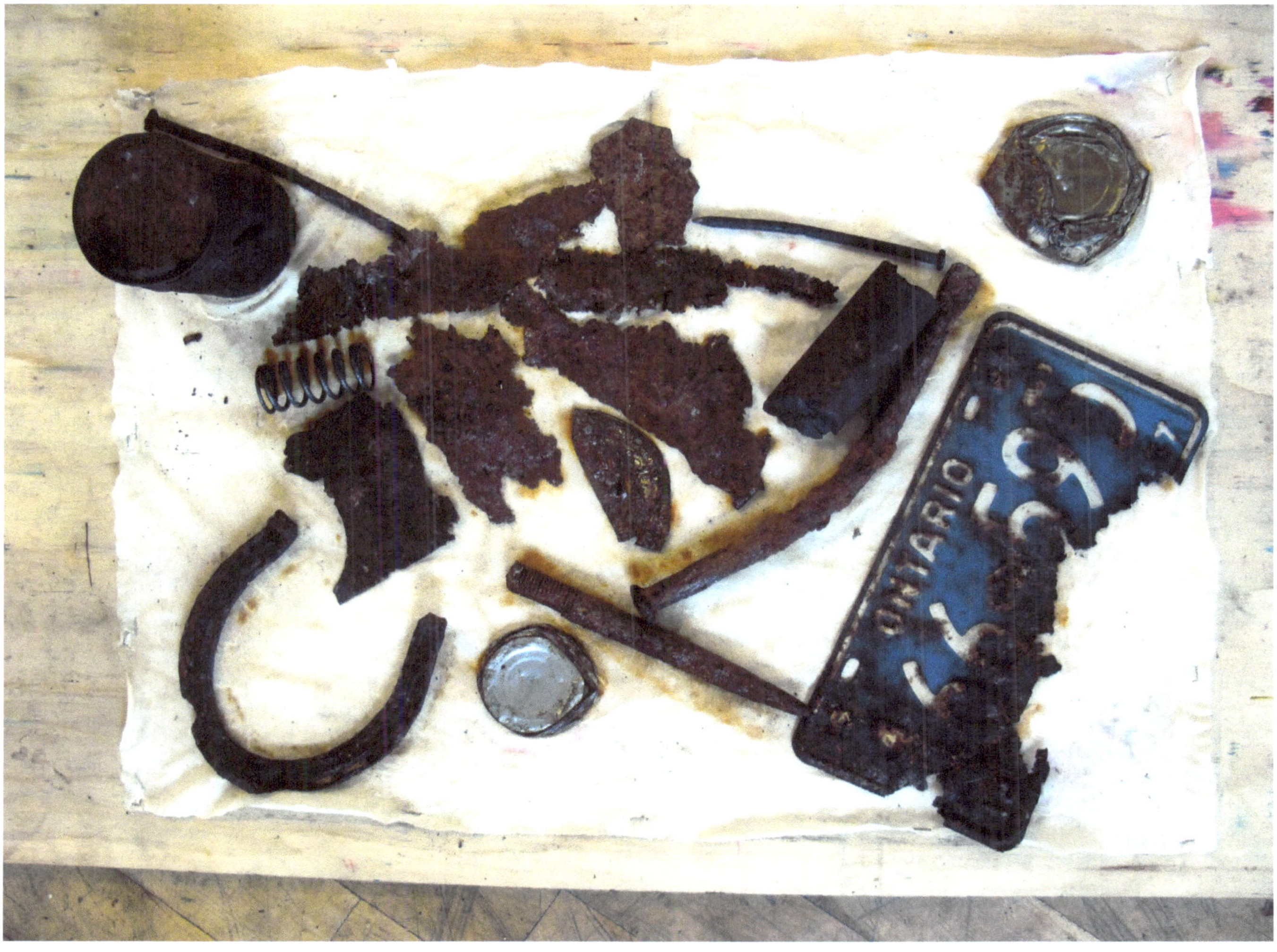

NIALL MCCLELLAND *Traces 1–4*, (in progress) 2012. Mixed media on cotton paper.

WHAT HAPPENS BETWEEN THE TWO
A (BRIEF) INTERVIEW WITH ARTIST KATE MCQUILLEN

Hannah King

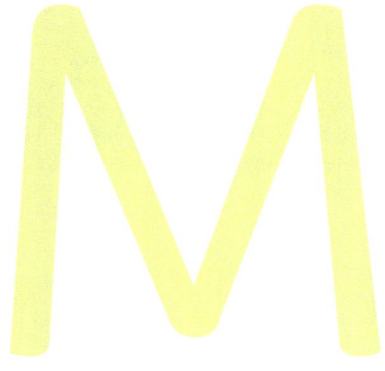

aterial Assumptions is an exhibition focusing on the many ways artists can use paper. When choosing the artists for this exhibition we paid special attention to artists who weren't necessarily using paper in their work, but who were making work we thought lent itself to the medium. Kate McQuillen was an exception. As a printmaker and a former artist-in-residence at the Center for Book and Paper Arts, Kate was already well versed in handmade paper and had used it in several projects. That she had this previous experience made her an interesting artist to me. Kate has a distinct perspective: she knows about handmade paper but doesn't use it as her primary medium, and she is also consistently concerned with the conceptual implications of the materials she uses. These two facts, to me, make her uniquely placed to make comment. Via e-mail, the following conversation was born.

HANNAH KING: So, the reasons why I chose you for this interview are many, but the big one is the diversity of materials that you use. There seems to be a strong connection between you as an artist, and the materials you use in your work. This is especially true in the pieces where you are using the subject matter as the medium [Smoke Paintings]. I'm really interested in your process and how your ideas develop. There also seems to be a labor-intensity in most everything you make, which, being a papermaker and printer myself, I really relate to. Could you tell me a little bit about your process?

KATE MCQUILLEN: Sometimes I get ideas when working directly with materials while at the shop, and sometimes I get them outside of the studio when doing something else entirely. Once something has popped into my head, I'll do a little research to see what else might interest me about that particular idea, and then I'll go back to reworking it in the studio. I'm always searching for materials or mediums that I think would

lend a conceptual layer to the work. I think about how the materials that bring the work into a physical form can have an effect, even subtly, on how the idea is received by the viewer.

For instance, for many years, I dealt with subject matter that had little-to-no physical form: cell-phone signals, electronic communications, etc. When trying to depict these things, I decided to use paper as a material, because of its link to the history of mass communication through printing, and its somewhat impermanent nature.

More recently, I've been working with ideas involving makeshift weapons. These are very real objects that inflict serious physical damage. I've had to move into other materials in order to depict these in the way I'd like: found objects, small metals, using smoke from matches like a paintbrush on paper, etc. In each piece, I feel that the idea pushed me toward the medium, and then something unexpected would unfold once I started working in that medium that would

push the project further.

KING: You've worked with handmade paper before in pieces such as *The Eagle Has Landed: Approach/Attack/Burial* and *Full Moons*. How do you find that working with handmade paper is different for you than working with machine made paper?

MCQUILLEN: Making paper from scratch has the major advantage of immediate sculptural possibilities. For years, in my pieces about telecommunications, I worked with printed machine made paper, laboring over scores, folds and cuts to get the material to the form that I'd like it to be. In *The Eagle Has Landed*, I had the opportunity to cut right to the chase, and arrive at a 3-dimensional form very quickly by simply sculpting the paper pulp. This allowed for more freedom and quick decision-making, which I feel gave the project more life.

In *The Eagle Has Landed*, I also had the ability to stress my conceptual reasons for using paper by purposefully giving the paper a chunky, rough appearance. I wanted to highlight the fantastic, childhood-dream aspect of the moon landing story by portraying it through obviously handmade means. I was also able to poke at ideas of faked moon landing conspiracy theories through my own, obvious fakery. The viewer is given just enough information to know that they are looking at an image of the moon; upon a slightly closer glance, though, they can see such recognizable details as the frayed paper fibers in the astronaut's spacesuits, illuminated by the spotlight, and the familiar crinkle of crumpled tin foil in the landing gear of the *Eagle*.

KING: Do you find that working with handmade paper influences the conceptual side of the work?

MCQUILLEN: The pieces I chose to make for this show reference x-ray imaging and surveillance in our post-9/11 environment. They depict articles of my own clothing with weapons planted within them, and are treated in a way that makes them look like x-rays. They depict [a] variety of weapons, some actually dangerous, and some that, though probably harmless, are banned from airplanes. With this show, I was very excited to make versions of these pieces using handmade paper, as the uneven and deckled edges seem to highlight the folds and creases of the skirts and blouses used in the works. I also liked the idea of printing on a fully cotton rag paper to reinforce the materiality of the clothing depicted in the works.

KING: When we approached you for this project you proposed several different ideas? How did the fact that they would be from handmade paper affect your proposed ideas (if at all)?

MCQUILLEN: Paper is often a medium of choice for me due to its versatility, and its ability as a sculptural material to also carry two-dimensional imagery. Blank and bare, it represents an everyday material that we use as scrap. Printed, it can carry images or data. It can be burned, folded, scored, cut up, glued. I feel it's a very loaded material with endless possibilities for application.

One of the works I proposed was a large installation piece, in which a paper fire extinguisher would be spraying forth paper pulp. This is an example of how sometimes I feel like I see the world through some sort of art-material-glasses; I clearly remember a day where I was walking past a fire extinguisher mounted on a wall, and suddenly had an image pop into my head of it shooting out paper pulp instead of that foamy stuff that's actually inside it. Perhaps it comes from working directly with materials day in and day out, or maybe it comes from generally having my head in the clouds most of the time, but I often amuse myself with these kinds of ideas. I like to make associations between similar materials, and then draw out ideas from what happens between the two.

Excerpted from an interview between the author and artist, April 28 – May 7, 2012

KATE MCQUILLEN *Skirt*, 2012. Pressure monoprint on cotton handmade paper. 22 x 30 inches.

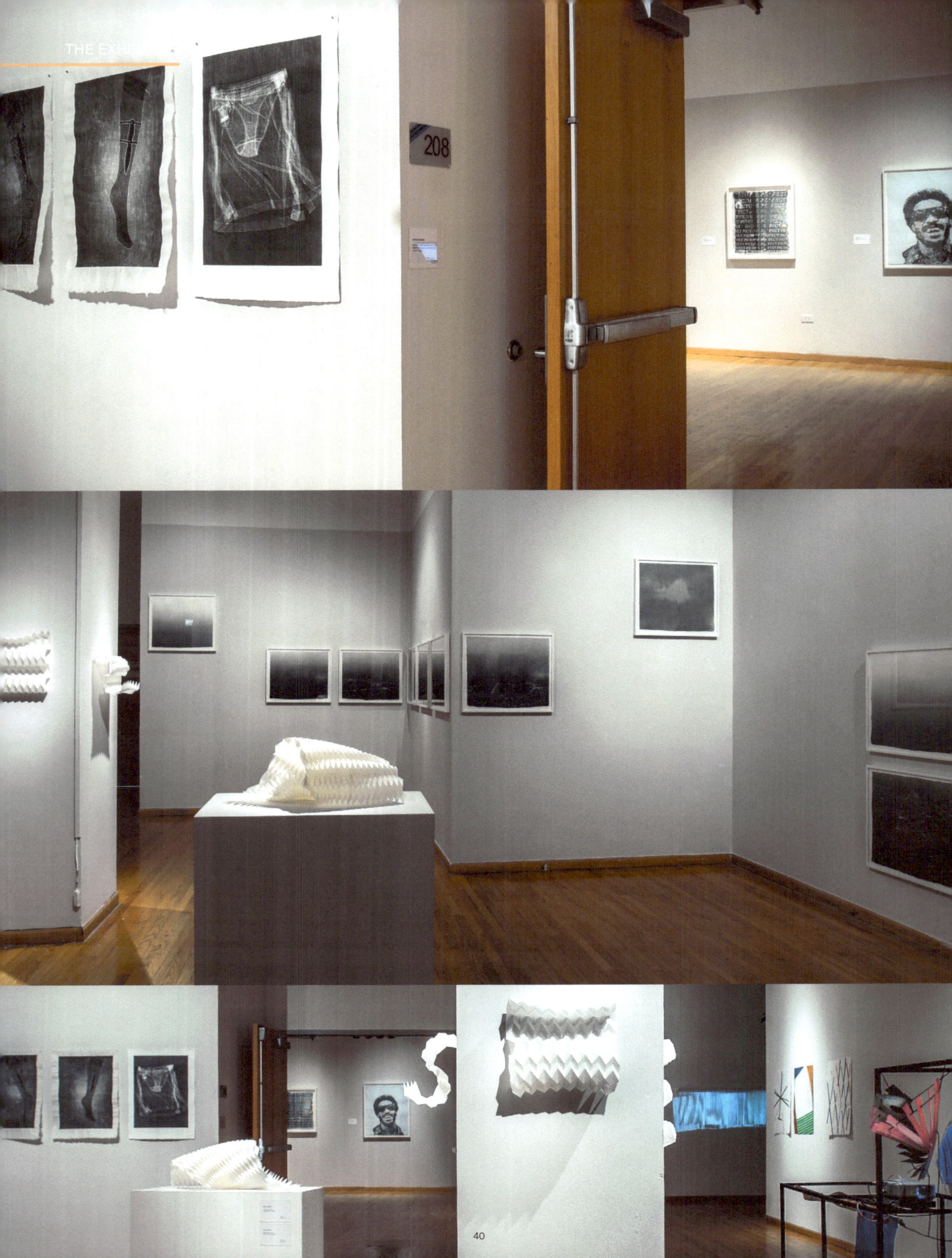

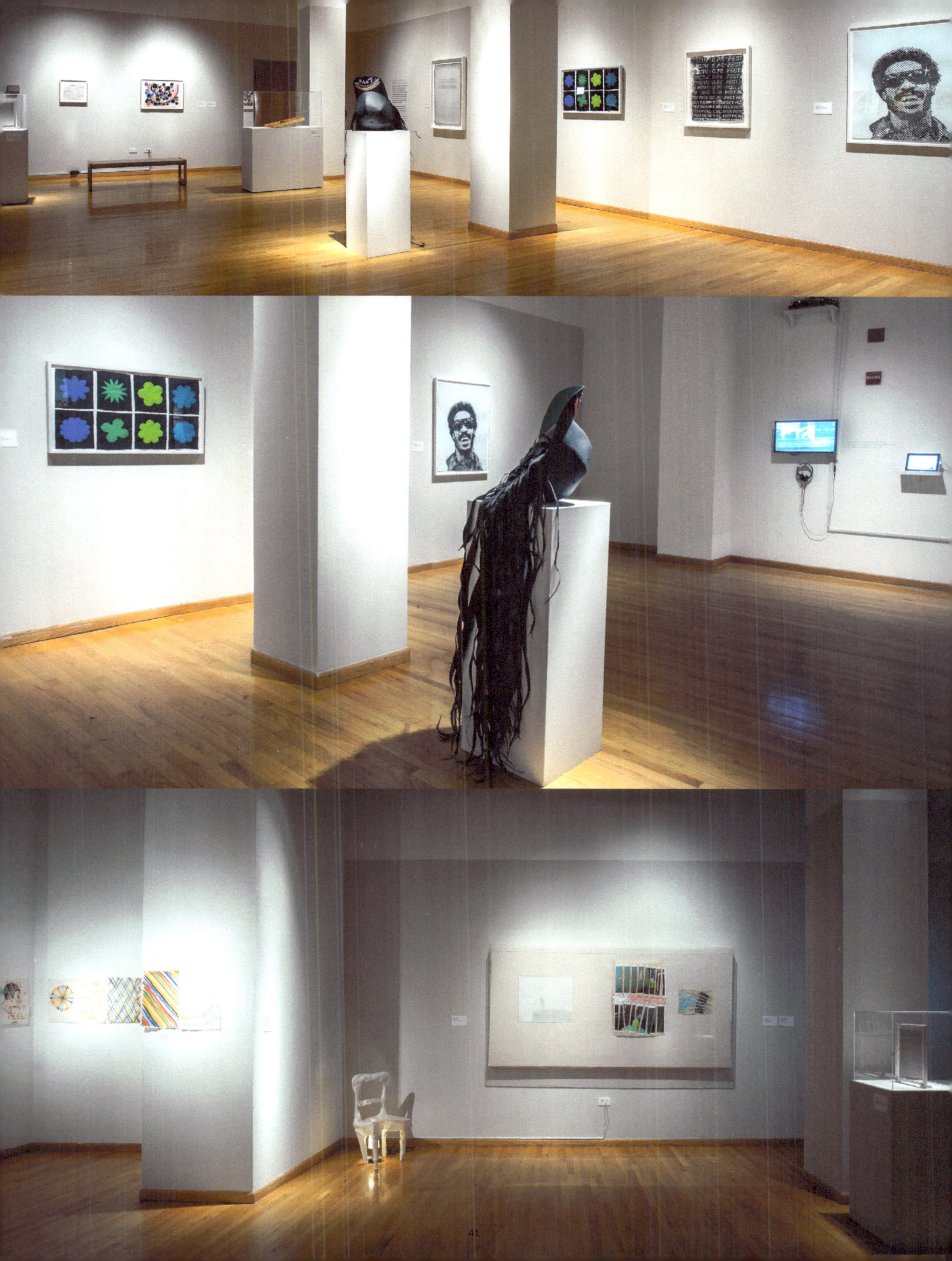

LANGUAGE IS NOT TRANSPARENTRENT
LANGUAGE IS NOT TRANSPARENT
LANGUAGE IS NOT TRANSPARENT
LANGUAGE IS NOT TRANSPARENT
LANGUAGE IS NOT TRANSPARENT
LANGUAGE IS NOT TRANSPARENT
LANGUAGE IS NOT TRANSPARENT

MEL BOCHNER *Language Is Not Transparent*, 1999 Watermarked translucent abaca on black cotton. 40 x 30 inches. Edition 11 /16.

ARTISTIC COLLABORATION AT DIEU DONNÉ

Dieu Donné was founded thirty-five years ago to further the field of handmade paper and to utilize collaboration to explore the untapped potential of this centuries-old medium as a contemporary art form. Intent on exploring the potential of handmade paper in new ways, Susan Gosin and Bruce Weinburg founded Dieu Donné in a small Soho loft in 1976. They quickly came to realize that matching diverse and innovative contemporary artists with skilled master papermakers would allow for seemingly endless experimentation in the medium. The excitement of bringing together these creative hands and minds ensured the old adage that the sum is great than its parts.

Traditionally, artistic practice can be a very solitary experience. At Dieu Donné, the artist is challenged with a different environment: a bustling studio, unfamiliar equipment and materials, and trained papermakers who have dedicated their careers to working in a medium developed over 2,000 years ago. The artist must approach an entirely new medium while sharing their very personal creative vision with a collaborator. Many of our artists have later confessed their initial anxiety and fear that they would be the first in our long history not to find a way to work in this unfamiliar medium. It just doesn't happen. Fear and failure are encouraged but supported. And, by sharing in the intimate process of creation, we begin to realize other rewards: the studio becomes a laboratory and the artists inspire our collaborators to push the boundaries of hand papermaking in new ways. The inherent unpredictability of the medium also plays a role, with unexpected outcomes often having extraordinary results. Exhilarated by the potential of paper and the challenge this opportunity presents, the Dieu Donné studio is alive—a wild and wet world of possibilities for the artist who has been energized by the creative confidence the medium and our collaborators bring to the process.

Former residency artist Ian Cooper (creator of *Chalice*, 2010) says it best:

My experience in the Workspace Residency played out like most 80s underdog action movies: at first I was all cocky, but right out of the gate, repeated experimentation failures left me bruised and battered. Dusting myself off, I listened to confidence building rock music and started hitting my marks. In the final showdown, I rose from the ashes (pulp) like some paper phoenix and realized a totally complex artwork that I couldn't be happier with, nor could I imagine it been made in any other way, or at any other facility.

We are honored to share our work with the Columbia College Center for Book and Paper Arts, and thankful to its staff and supporters for this wonderful opportunity. By sharing a small but significant sample of the works created by over 800 artists who have worked in collaboration in our "wet studio," we hope that those viewing this exhibition will begin to experience the vast possibilities that exist through collaboration in this ever-evolving medium.

Kathleen Flynn
Executive Director, Dieu Donné
April 2012

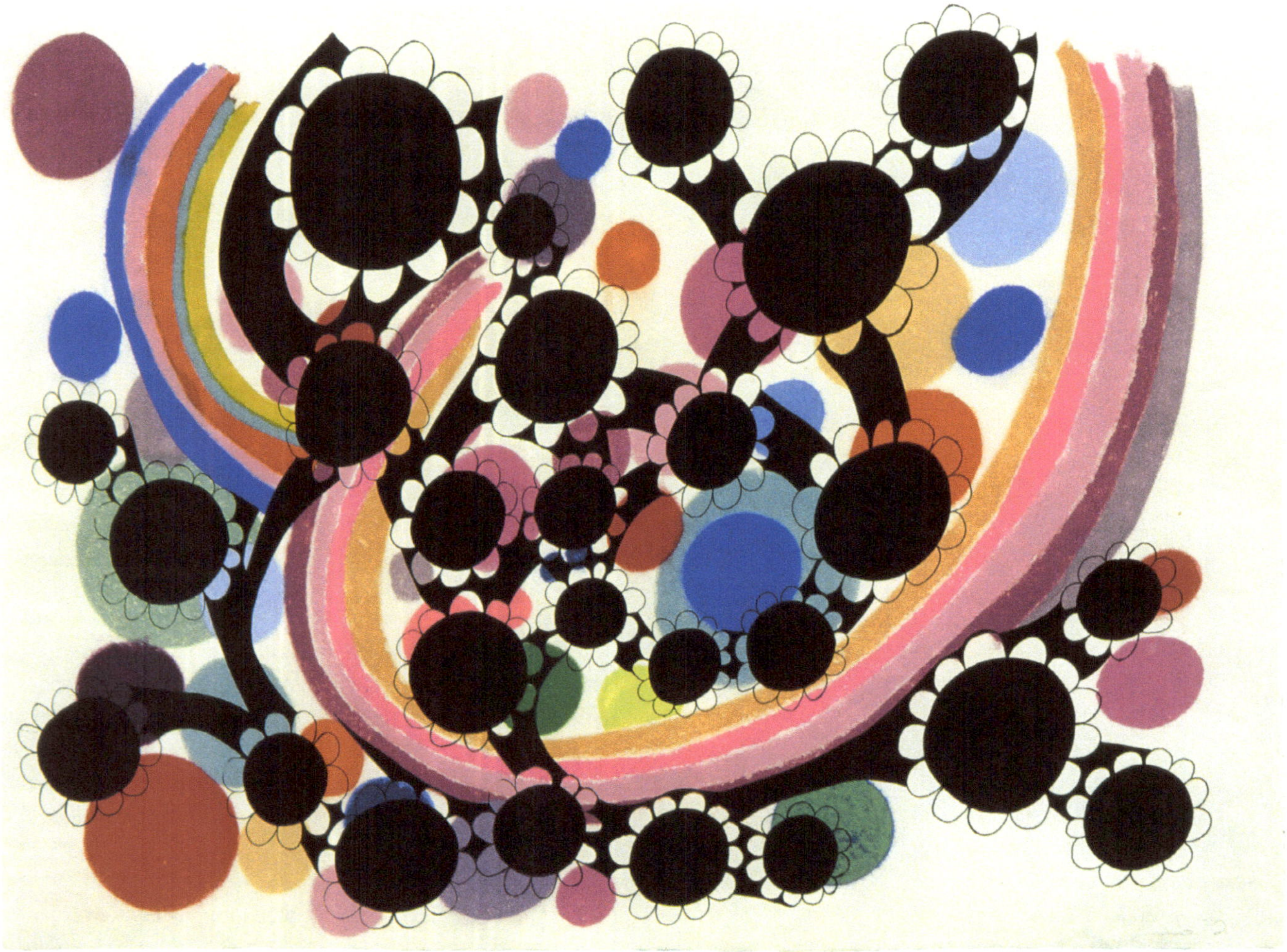

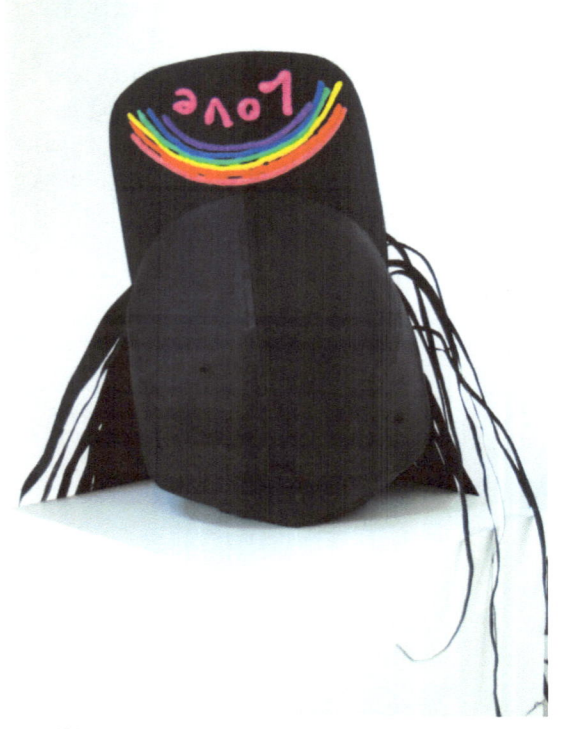

NINA BOVASSO *Black Flowers with Rainbow Colors*, 2006. Cotton base sheet with cotton pulp painting and screenprint. 18 x 24 inches. Edition of 100, AP3/10.

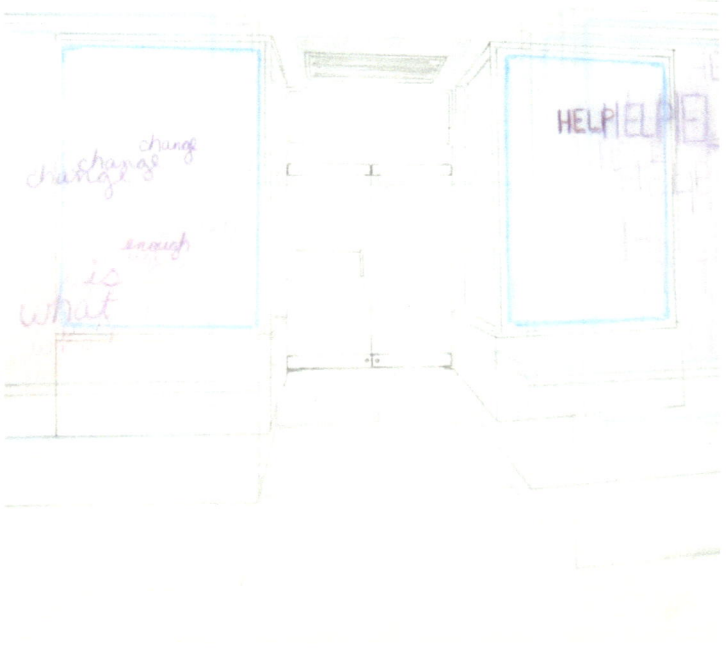

IAN COOPER *Chalice*, 2010. Handmade denim and cotton papers, commercial papers, fabric, cast paper pulp, trash bags, brush bristles, gloss medium, and jade adhesive. 57 x 11 x 16 inches.

BETH CAMPBELL *Potential Store Fronts Sketch*, 2007. Ink and colored pencil on abaca. 12 x 12 inches.

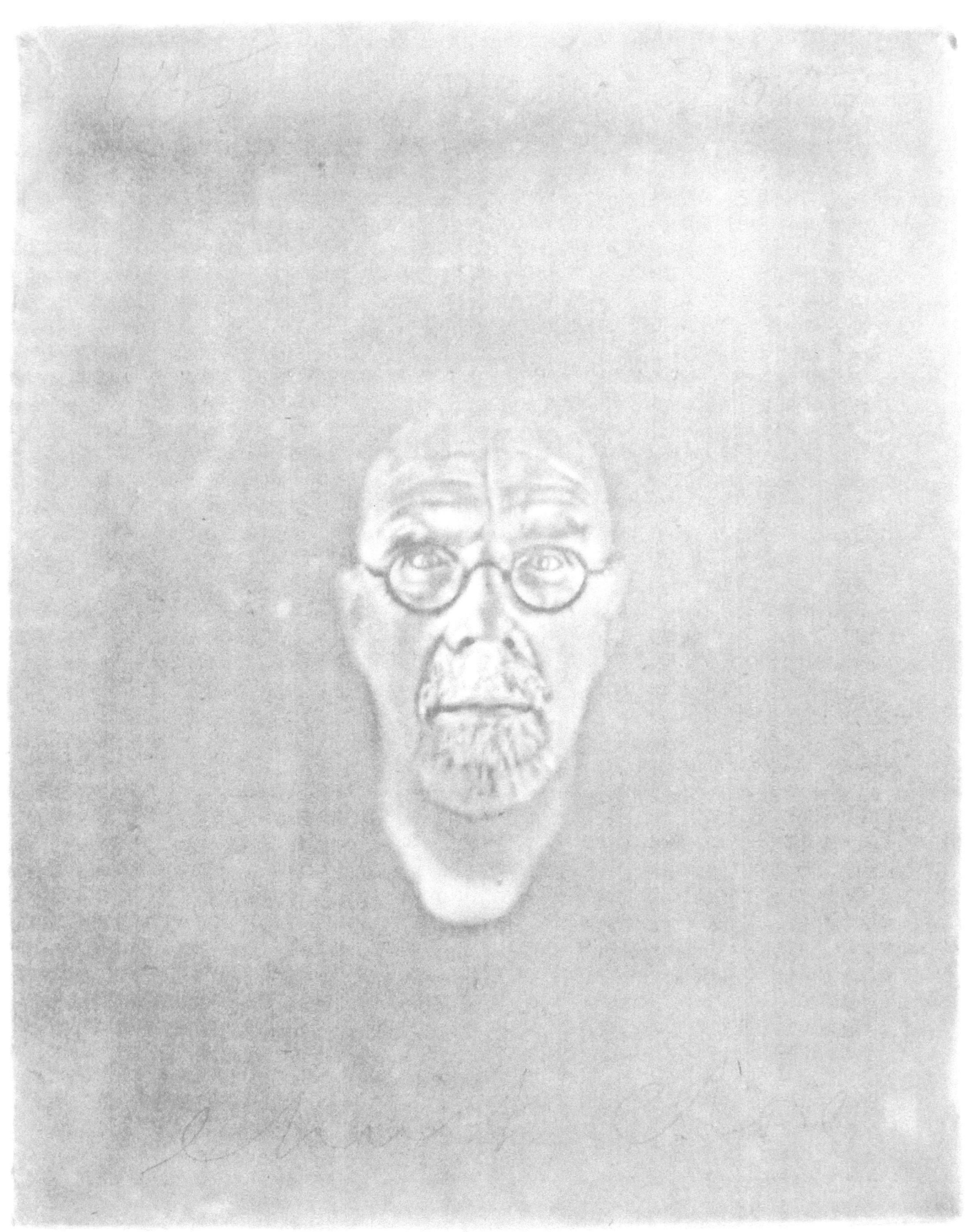

CHUCK CLOSE *Watermark Self-Portrait*, 2007. Light and shade watermark, abaca and cotton fiber pigmented with carbon black. 11 3/4 x 9 1/4 inches. Edition 3/35.

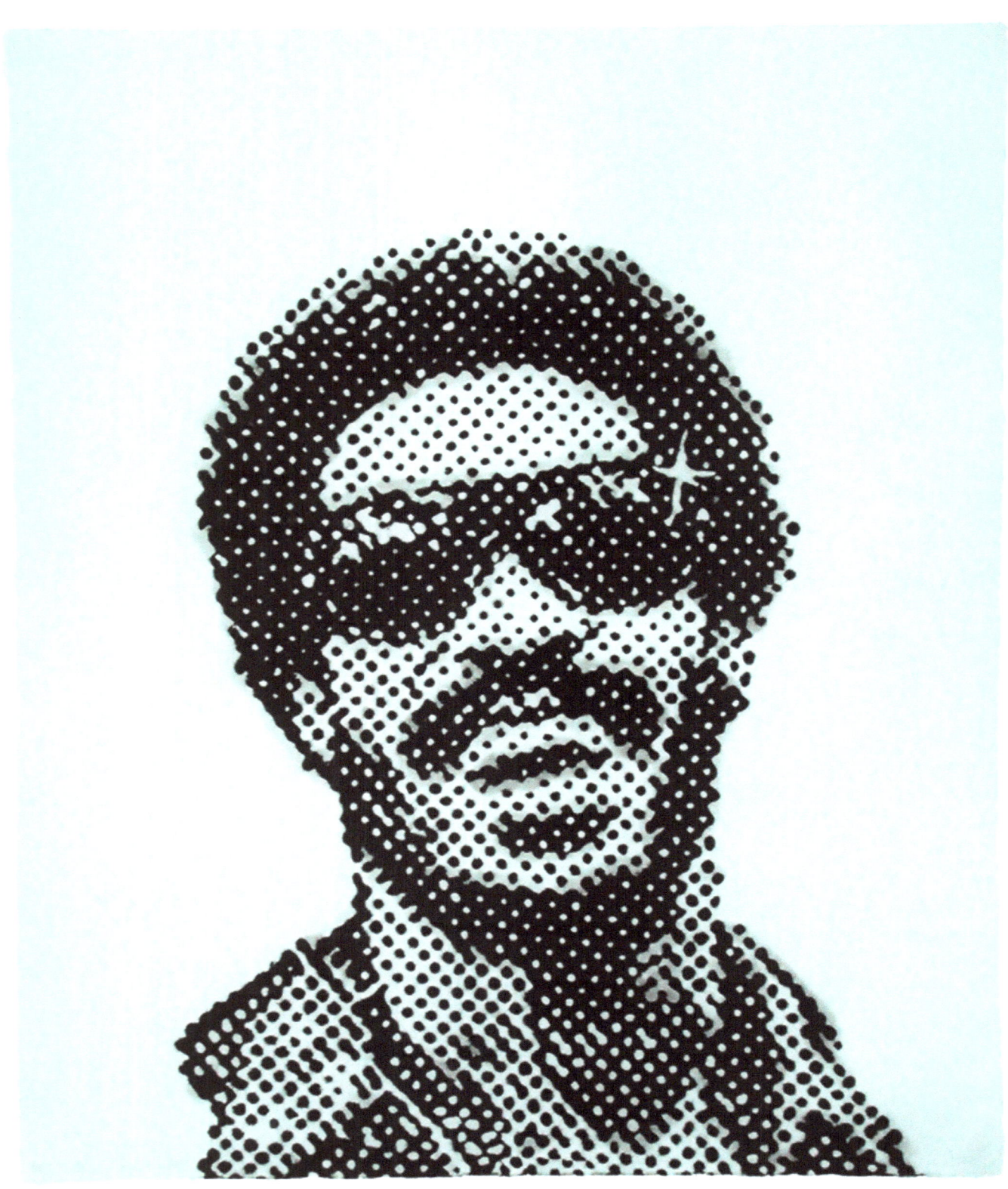

GLENN LIGON *Self Portrait at Eleven Years Old*, 2004. Cotton base sheet with stenciled linen pulp painting. 36 x 30 inches. DD 1/5.

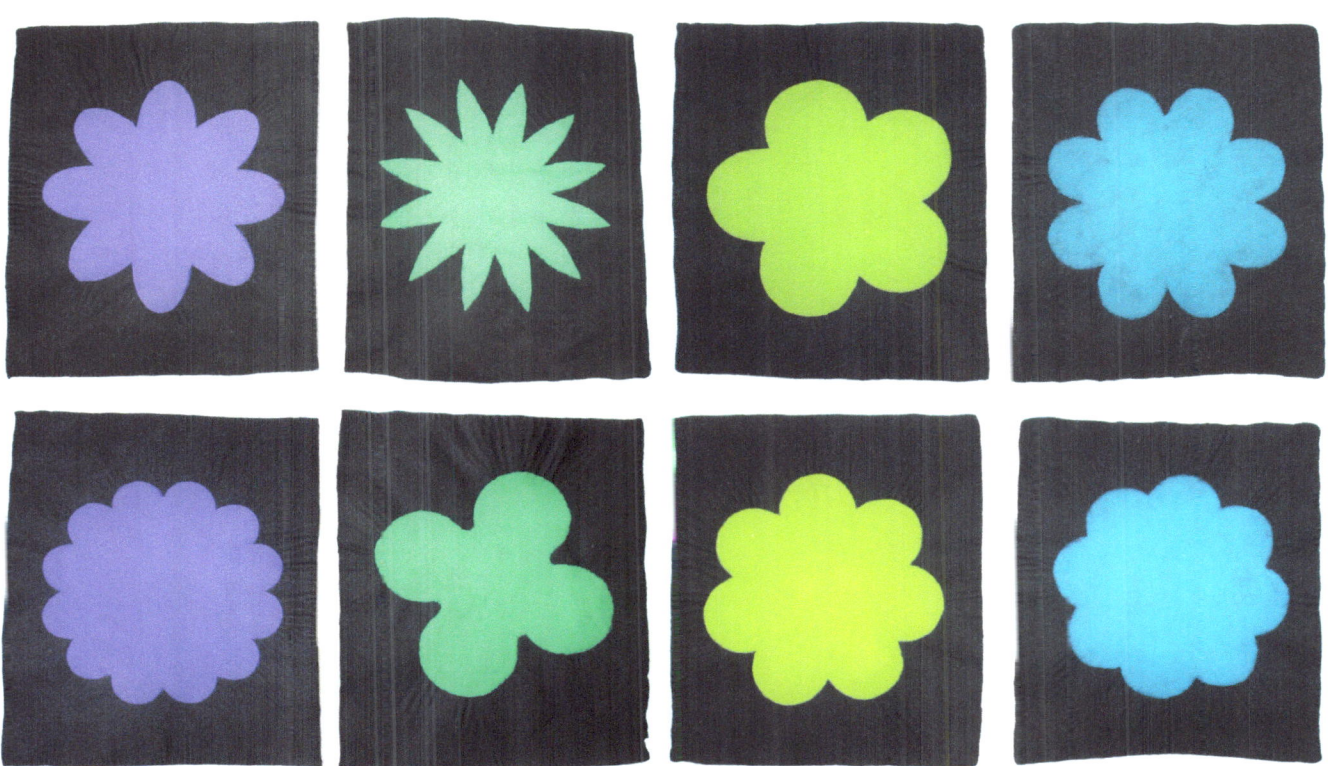

FOLLY APFELBAUM *Power to the Flower*, 2007. Stenciled linen pulp paint on abaca; color and shape vary. 10 x 8 inches. Edition of 50, PCP1/2.

SONYA BLESOFSKY *Broadway Development Williamsburg 2006 II*, 2007. Pigmented abaca on pigmented cotton. 18 x 22 inches. Unique.

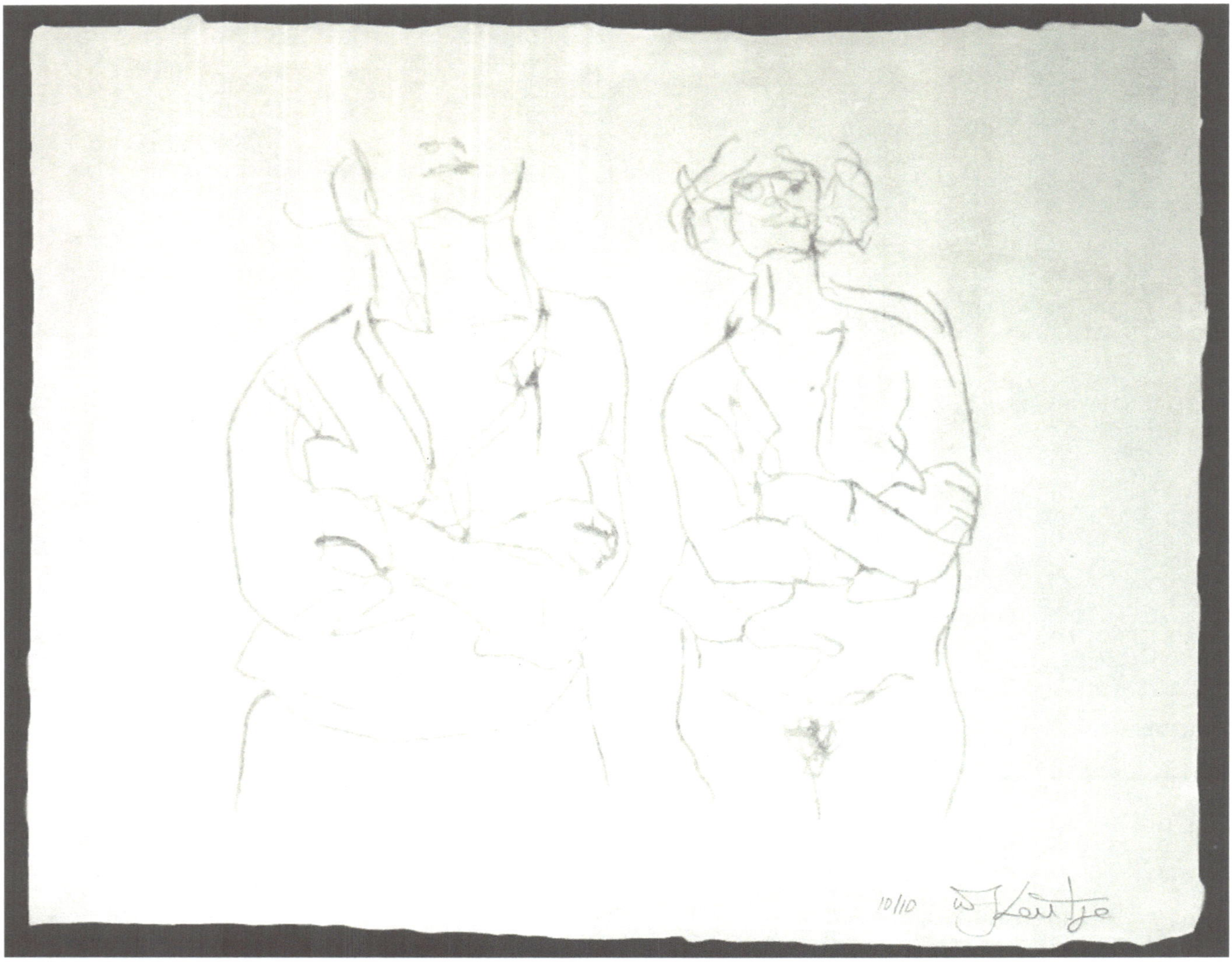

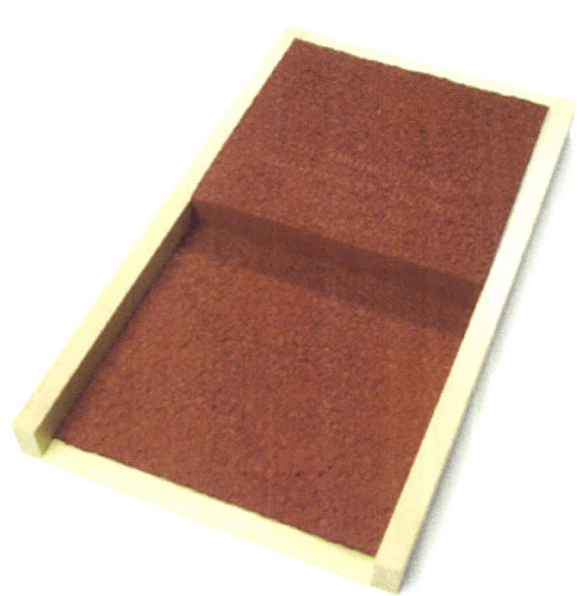

WILLIAM KENTRIDGE *Anne*, 2009. Watermarked cotton. 11 x 14 inches. Edition 3/10.

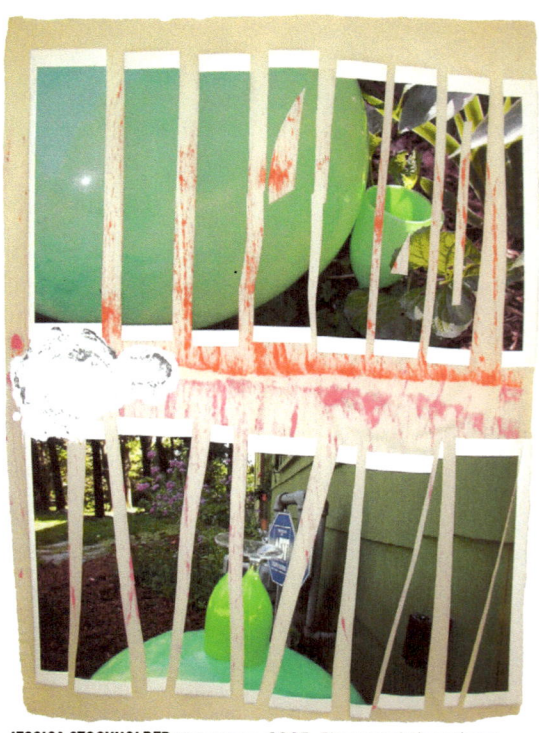

RICHARD TUTTLE *Entertaining...*, 2002. Sugar pine with satin polyurethane finish, maple plywood, letterpress on pigmented, embossed cotton paper. 20 x 11 1/2 x 1 1/2 inches. Edition # DDP 2/3.

JESSICA STOCKHOLDER *Violet Haze*, 2005. Pigmented abaca base sheet with pulp painting and archival inkjet print. 22 x 30 inches. Unique work.

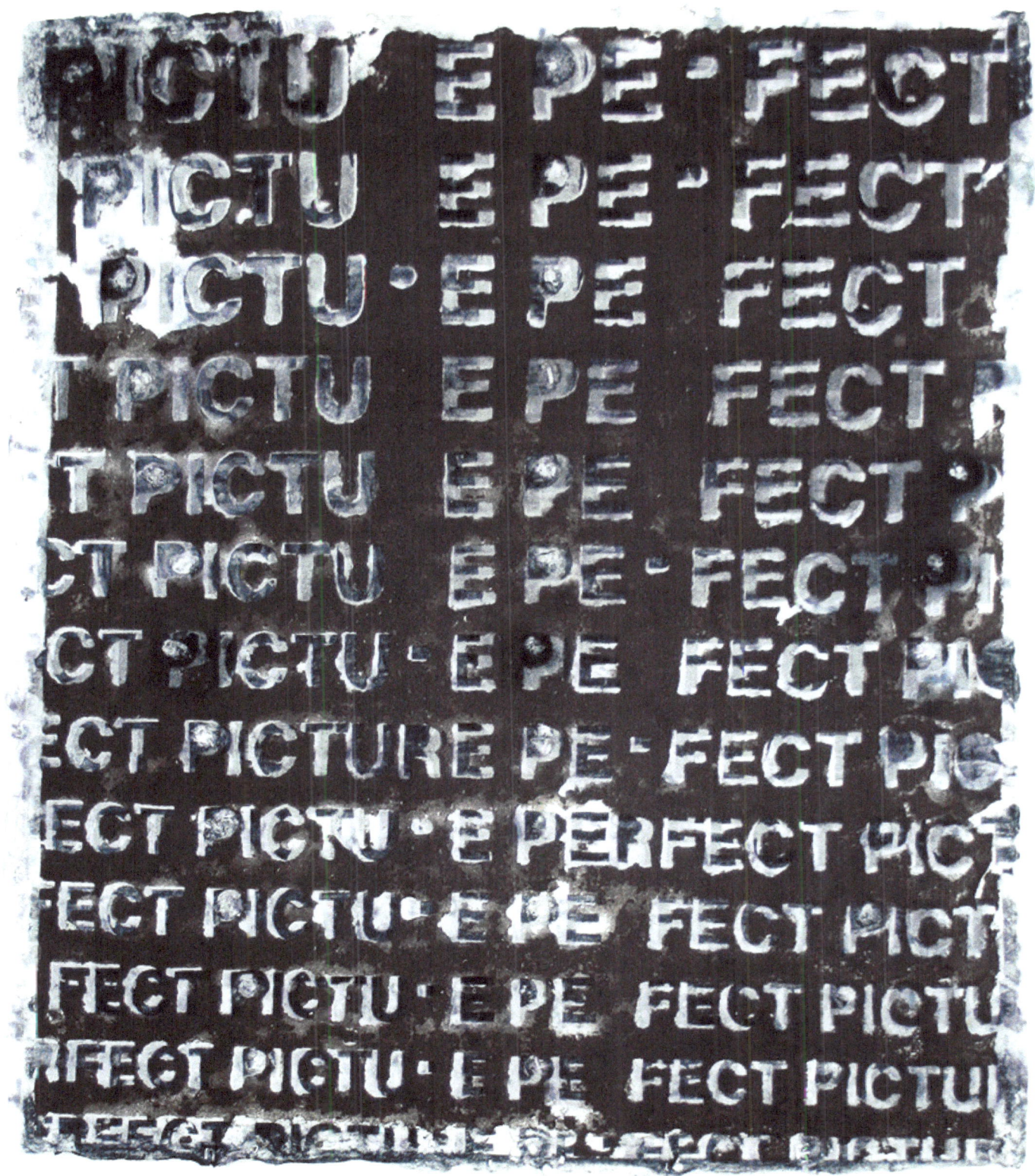

MATT KEEGAN *Picture Perfect (Monoprint #3,*, 2010. Stenciled pigmented linen pulp on cotton handmade paper. 26.5 x 22.5 inches. Unique work.

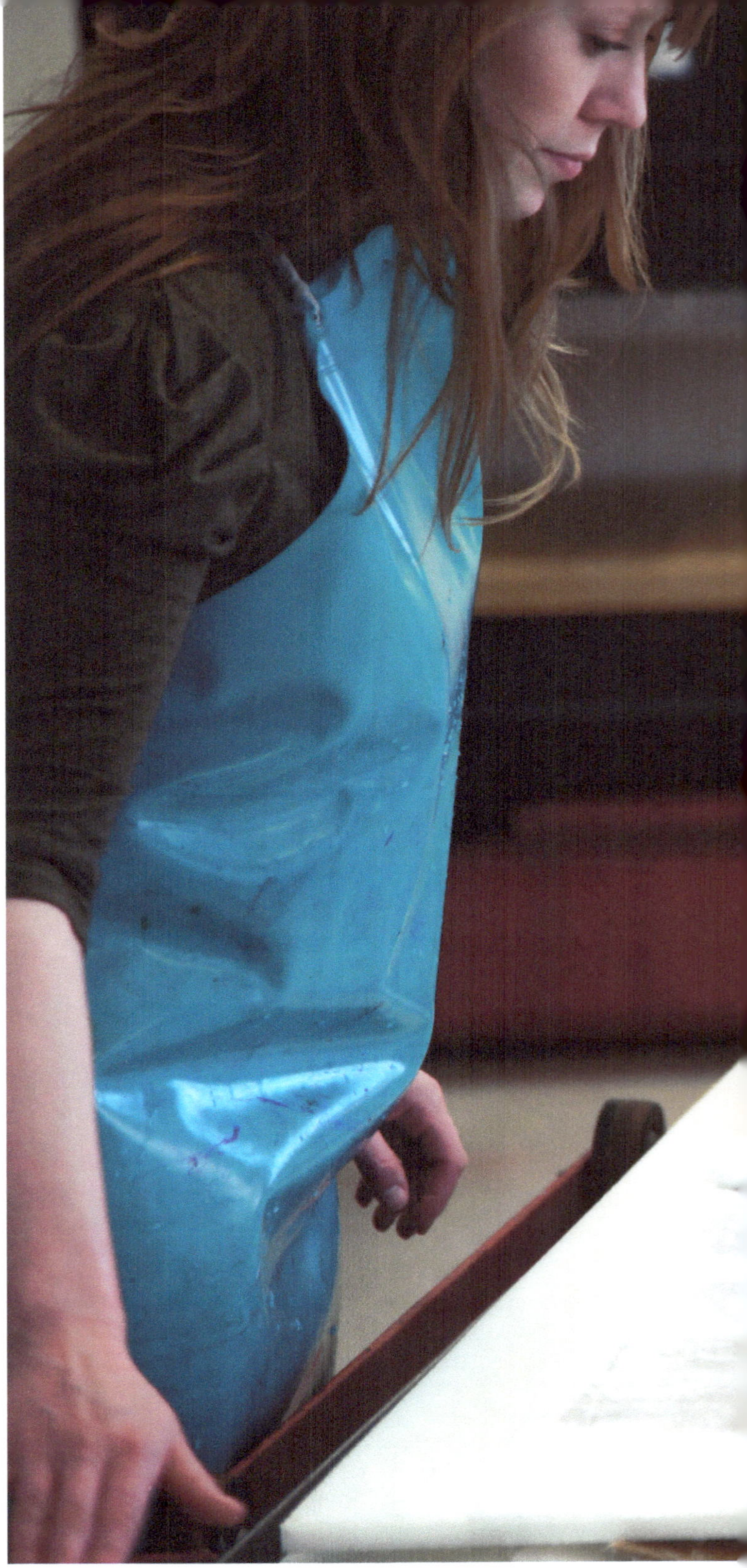

LABOR, PROCESS, DIALOGUE: HAND PAPERMAKING AS COLLABORATIVE MODEL

Elizabeth Isakson-Dado

> Collaboration, in its diffusion of individual authorship, places the emphasis less on the who and more on the what. For us, working together makes public a commitment to the process of exchange that goes on whether it is an individual or group effort. Most important, collaborating is more satisfying than working alone.

ANN HAMILTON AND KATHRYN CLARK, *VIEW*, 1991

Collaboration is an integral part of hand papermaking in a studio environment, whether it is with master papermakers at a studio like Dieu Donné, or in my experience as a graduate student learning the craft as the basis for my own artwork. Many contemporary artists, like Ann Hamilton and Kathryn Clark, consider the process of collaboration increasingly important to a contemporary art practice because it fosters a dialogue that aids to a deeper connection to concept as well as to craft. As a way to focus more clearly on methodology behind the medium of paper, my co-curators Jessica Cochran, Hannah King, C. J. Mace, and I decided to work collaboratively, not only with each other, but also with the thirteen artists we chose to exhibit in *Material Assumptions*. We created paper in our studio that was directly tied to the concerns of each individual artwork, and through that specific attention, we could provide the artist with a tailored raw material to serve as the impetus for their piece. This handmade connection—creating the visual starting point—drew us further into each artist's intention; and as artists communicated their projects to us through proposals and emails, we gained a deeper sense of what the commissioned work would be, and how we would choose to arrange the work as curators in the gallery.

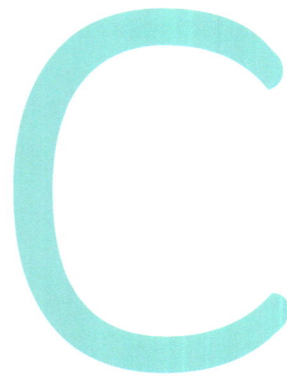

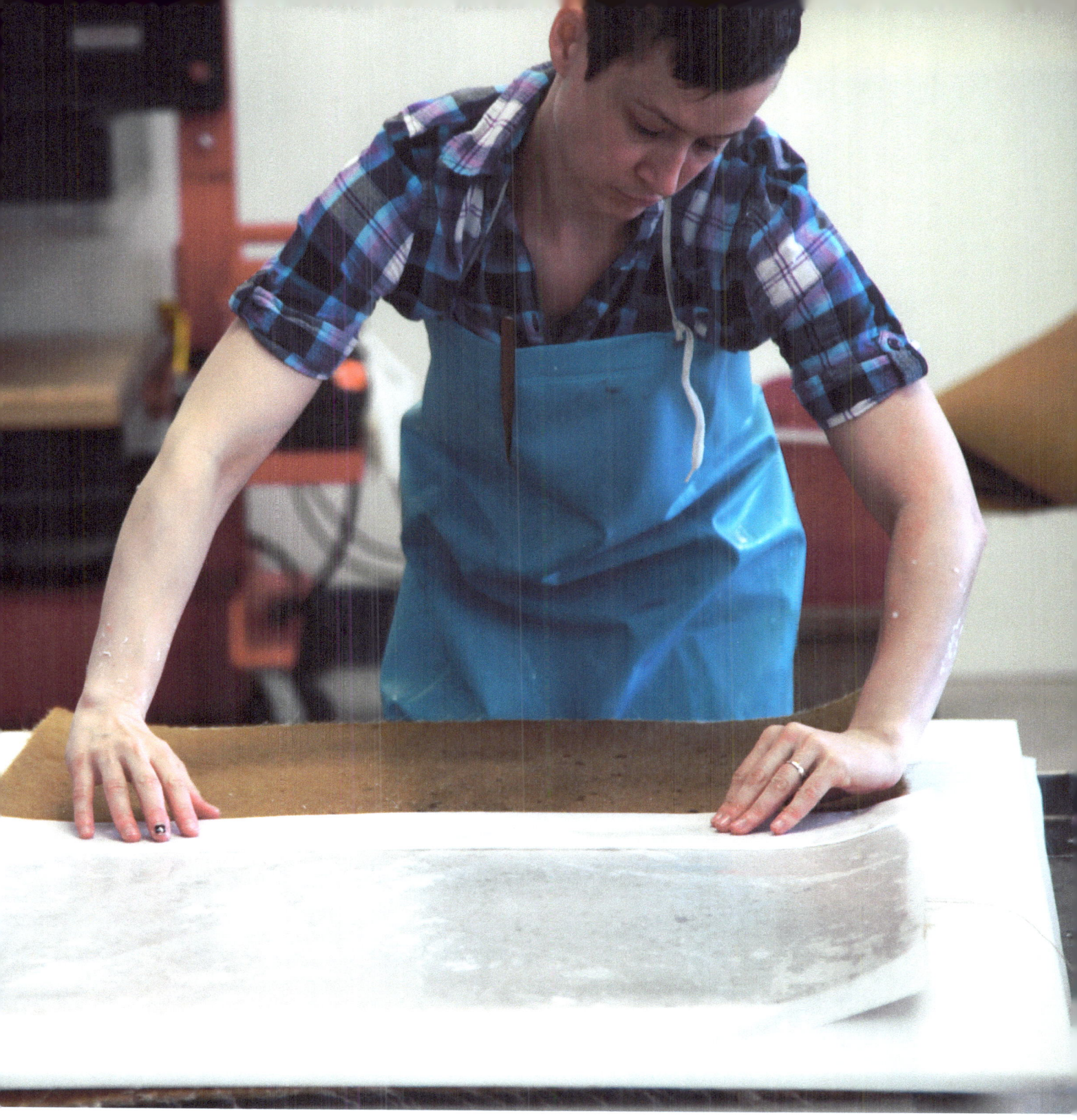

In *Material Assumptions*, my co-curators and I collaborated on multiple levels, and each stage became a complex conversation: choosing artists to participate in the show, finalizing the fibers to use in the handmade paper, weighing the choices the artists would have in finished sheets, devising a strategy to make samples so artists could easily understand the material, negotiating the need of each artist based on his or her vision and proposal—but most of all, making all the various types and sizes of paper

requested, by hand. We approached and executed these tasks with mutual responsibility, and the four of us quickly learned how to work together in a way that opened up the possibilities for the exhibition.

As artists, Hannah, C. J., and I work in the paper studio at the Center for Book and Paper Arts to carry out our personal work, usually making paper alongside our colleagues, but remaining

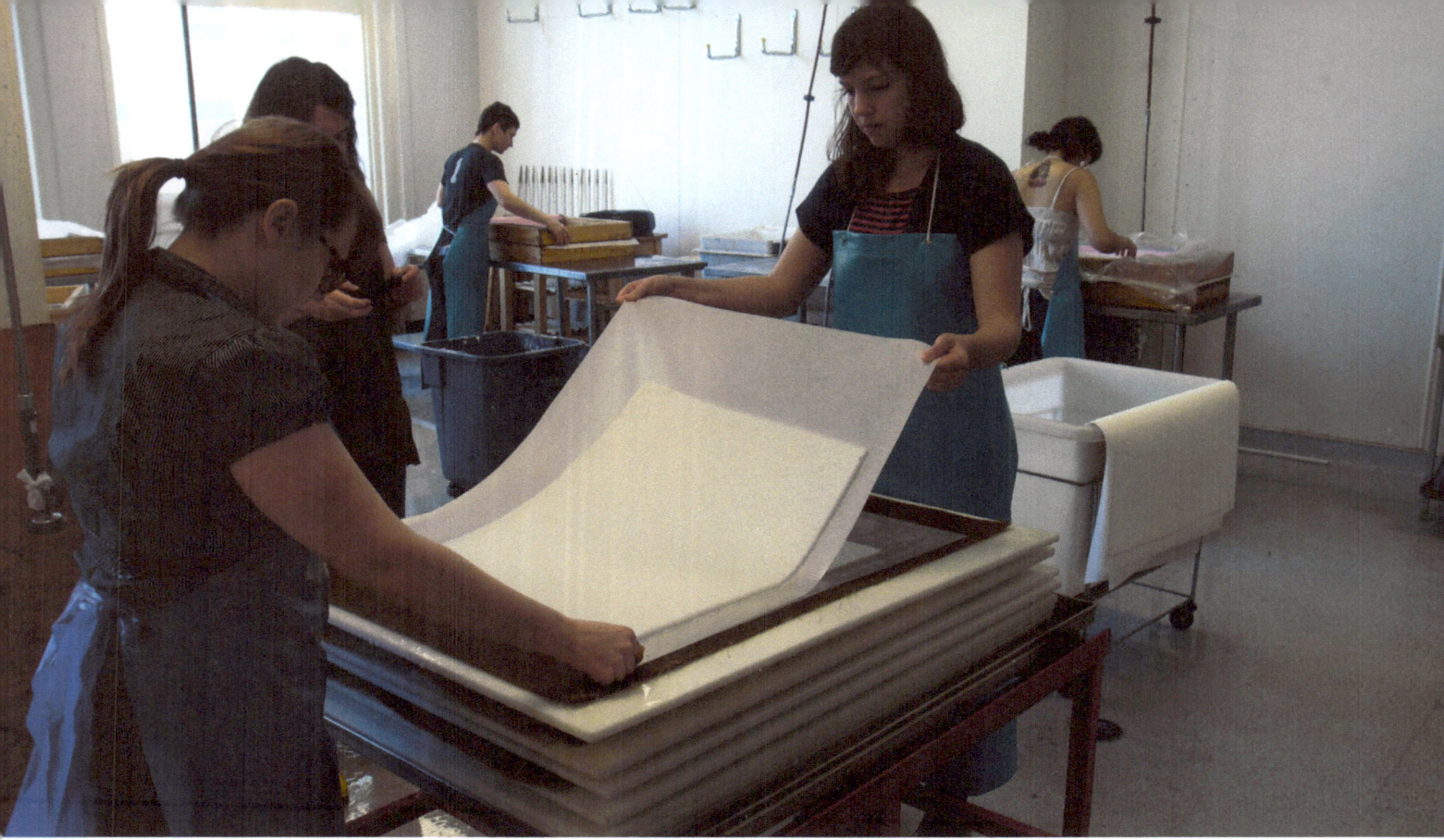

focused on our individual pieces rather than collaboration. As part of a papermaking course, we have each worked with visiting artists to assist in producing an edition of handmade paper, but the scale has been quite small in comparison to the scope of a studio like Dieu Donné. Facing a project as large as *Material Assumptions* became an exciting endeavor, and our process-based approach to art making began to directly inform the way we worked together as curators and papermaking collaborators for this project. It is a rare experience as a curator to work so closely with materials before the selected artists have made the finished work. Hannah, C. J., and I carefully beat the cotton and abaca fiber to the correct consistency, formed sheets of various thicknesses and sizes, and chose the best method to dry the paper according to each artist's proposal. The papermaking ritual became a collaborative model for us, and strengthened our relationship to the material through the labor of craft.

My co-curators and I also engaged in a rigorous studio dialogue that has shaped the final outcome of the exhibition, beginning at the material level. Each artist proposed working with paper in a different way, and our methods in the studio had to be flexible enough to change with each individual artist's need. For example, we were acutely aware that the thin, translucent abaca we made for paper engineer Matt Shlian would directly affect his intricately folded origami forms. We chose to form Shlian's paper in a large deckle box and then cut the pieces down to size, so the final product could be as consistently thin as possible. In my conversation with Ian Schneller, we discussed the specific need for thick, absorbent sheets of cotton paper to allow him to easily mold the paper into sculptural, audio horn speakers. We pulled Schneller's paper by hand with a mould and deckle from un-sized cotton and created several extra sheets, in case he needed more room for trial and error with the new material. To accommodate proposals for large installations, including Susan Goethel Campbell's matrix of detailed relief prints and Anna Tsantir's wall of overlapping sheets of abaca, we had to dedicate an entire day in the studio to each artist and keep in constant communication about our progress. For Campbell's piece, which required thirty 20" x 24" sheets, four of us worked at our own deckle box station to form cotton sheets identical in texture, with a fifth papermaker checking for the quality and consistency of the sheets. Tsantir's proposal called for a large quantity as well as a custom size, so we built custom moulds that allowed us to form two sheets at once in an oversized

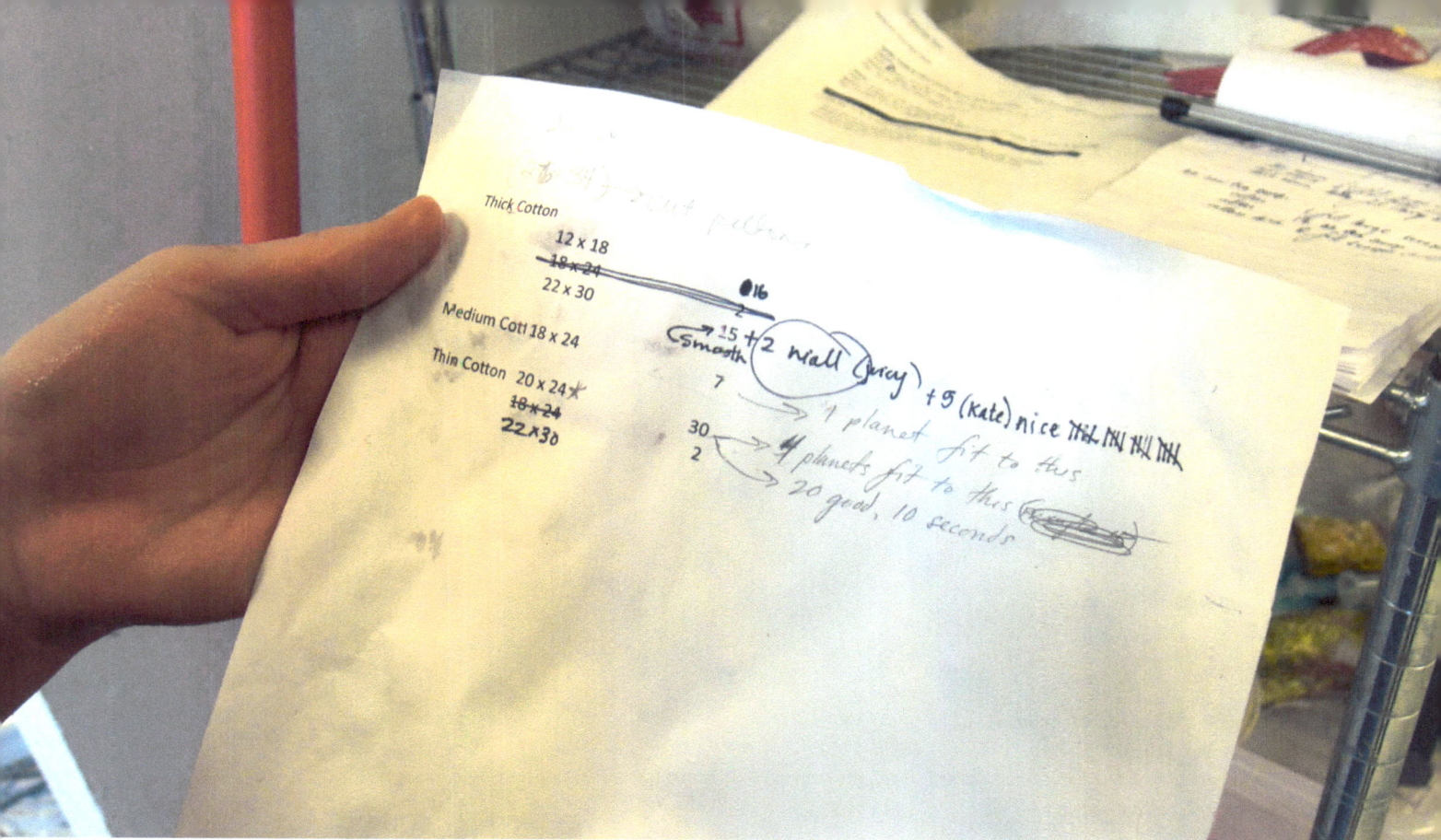

Photo by Jessica Cochran

deckle box, a process that took three of us to execute correctly each time, but greatly eased the total work load. Ultimately, the planning, consideration, and implementation of each artist's request resulted in more than one hundred sheets of handmade paper, formed from fifty pounds of pulp, over the course of just five days.

For me, *Material Assumptions* has been an educational exercise and a dialogue through making that has informed the final exhibition. As artists, Hannah, C. J., and I know that a connection to material is fundamental to the outcome of an artwork. Making paper for the participating artists has brought us closer to understanding their intention, and hopefully, their connection to the work is deepened by our conversations with one another and our collaborative effort to supply our skilled craft. As Ann Hamilton and Kathryn Clark proclaimed in their artists' statement for *View*, "In this, the work is both the labor and the thing." For us, the process of exchange is the dialogue around making, and communicating that process from hand papermaker to artist to curator is integral to the success of the *Material Assumptions* exhibition.

Ann Hamilton and Kathryn Clark, *View* (Washington, D.C.: Hirshhorn Museum and Sculpture Garden, Smithsonian Institution, 1991). In *Theories and Documents of Contemporary Art, A Sourcebook of Artists Writings*, compiled by Kristine Stiles and Peter Selz (Berkley: University of California Press, 1996), 625–26.

EXHIBITION CHECKLIST

Annica Cuppetelli & Cristobal Mendoza
Double Interference, 2012
Handmade cotton paper, MDF, computer, video
projector, camera, custom software
Dimensions variable

Deborah Boardman
Notes to the Beloved and Other Remarks, 2012
Gouache and mixed media on handmade
cotton and abaca paper
Dimensions variable

Susan Goethel Campbell
Other Cities:1–10, 2012
Relief prints with perforations on handmade
cotton paper
20 x 24 inches each
Unique works

Dan Devening
Untitled 1–3, 2012
Acrylic and collage on paper
30 x 32 inches

Daniel Luedtke
Birthday Girl, 2012
Mixed media installation
Dimensions variable

Niall McClelland
Traces 1–4, 2012
Mixed media on cotton paper
22 x 29 inches (1–3)
18 x 26 inches (4)

Kate McQuillen
Skirt, 2012
Pressure monoprint on cotton handmade paper
22 x 30 inches

Kate McQuillen
Hose, 2012
Pressure monoprint on abaca handmade paper
22 x 30 inches

Kate McQuillen
Tights, 2012
Pressure monoprint on abaca handmade paper
22 x 30 inches

Zoe Nelson
Her Holes II, 2012
Handmade cotton and abaca paper,
mixed media
12 x 9 x 6 inches

Julie Schenkelberg
Echo, 2012
Abaca handmade paper, glue, and lamp
with handmade shade
17 x 14 x 30 inches

Ian Schneller
White Hornlets, 2012
Handmade cotton paper, mixed media
19 x 19 x 5 inches

Matthew Shlian
Pleat Studies 1–5, 2012
Handmade cotton paper
Dimensions variable

Anna Tsantir
The Raven and the Wolf, 2012
Handmade abaca paper, string
Dimensions variable

FROM THE
DIEU DONNÉ ARCHIVE

Polly Apfelbaum
Power to the Flower, 2007
Stenciled linen pulp paint on abaca;
color and shape vary
10 x 8 inches
Edition of 50, PCP1/2

Sonya Blesofsky
Broadway Development Williamsburg 2006 II,
2007
Pigmented abaca on pigmented cotton
18 x 22 inches
unique

Mel Bochner
Language Is Not Transparent, 1999
Watermarked translucent abaca
on black cotton
40 x 30 inches
Edition 11/16

Nira Bovasso
Black Flowers with Rainbow Colors, 2006
Cotton base sheet with cotton pulp painting
and screenprint
18 x 24 inches
Edition of 100, AP3/10

Beth Campbell
Potential Store Fronts Sketch, 2007
Ink and colored pencil on abaca
12 x 12 inches

Chuck Close
Watermark Self-Portrait, 2007
Light and shade watermark, abaca and cotton
fiber pigmented with carbon black
11 3/4 x 9 1/4 inches
Edition 3/35

Ian Cooper
Chalice, 2010
Handmade denim and cotton papers,
commercial papers, fabric, cast paper pulp,
trash bags, brush bristles, gloss medium, and
jade adhesive
57 x 11 x 16 inches

Matt Keegan
Picture Perfect (Monoprint #3), 2010
Stenciled pigmented linen pulp
on cotton handmade paper
26.5 x 22.5 inches
unique

William Kentridge
Anne, 2009
Watermarked cotton
11 x 14 inches
Edition 3/10

Glenn Ligon
Self Portrait at Eleven Years Old, 2004
Cotton base sheet with stenciled
linen pulp painting
36 x 30 inches
DD 1/5

Jessica Stockholder
Violet Haze, 2005
Pigmented abaca base sheet with pulp
painting and archival inkjet print
22 x 30 inches
unique work

Jessica Stockholder
ADT, 2005
Collage
11 x 14 inches
unique work

Jessica Stockholder
On the Ledge, 2005
Collage
11 x 14 inches
unique work

Richard Tuttle
Entertaining... 2002
Sugar pine with satin polyurethane finish,
maple plywood, letterpress on pigmented,
embossed cotton paper
20 x 11 1/2 x 1 1/2 inches
Edition # DDP 2/3

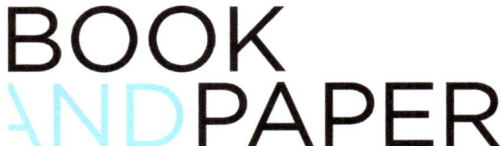

BOOK
ANDPAPER

CENTER FOR BOOK AND PAPER ARTS
at Columbia College Chicago

1104 SOUTH WABASH AVENUE, 2ND FLOOR
CHICAGO, ILLINOIS 60605
312 369 6630

COLUM.EDU/BOOKANDPAPER

create...
change

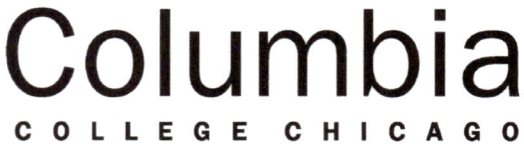

Columbia
COLLEGE CHICAGO

ISBN 978-0-929911-44-1

90000

9 780929 911441